Food Storage: Preserving Meat, Dairy, and Eggs

Susan Gregersen ~ David Armstrong

Special thanks to Pam Ritter and J D Smith
for their contributions.

David and I would both like to thank our families
for their patience and support as we wrote, researched,
and experimented with the things in this book!

Table of Contents

Introduction

(Susan)

This book isn't about how-to select and buy food storage. It's about what to do with the food once you've got it; how to preserve and store it. Even those who have been canning, freezing, or otherwise preserving food might find something here that they can use. I've been preserving food for over 30 years, but I still learn something new when I read another book or talk with a fellow food preserver.

There are already a lot of books about food preservation but what we've done to make this one unique is to take each food, one by one, and write about all the ways it can be preserved and how to do each one. It's frustrating to read a book about canning and most of them just have a chart where you can look up your food and get things like time and pressure for canning, or whether it needs to be blanched before freezing, and not a lot of specific information for that particular food.

In this book you can select the name of the food you're interested in preserving and go right to a whole section on just that food, with each preservation process explained as to how you use it for that food. For example, if you're about to butcher rabbits and you wonder what all ways you could preserve them, find 'rabbits' on the table of contents, turn to that page, and there it is, how to can, dehydrate, freeze, brine, smoke, and pickle them.

The first part of this book is an explanation of each of the food preserving techniques, how to do it and what you need to do it. For example, if you want to learn about smoking food, you can click on that subject and go right to the information on smoking food.

The next volume of this series, "Preserving Fruits, Nuts, and

Seeds", published in August 2013, is set up the same way. We hope to follow it with "Preserving Vegetables, Grains, and Beans" over the winter, 2013/2014.

I love to experiment and I've canned and dried some unusual things, like cooked oatmeal, or eggs. Some things worked, some didn't. Along the way I met a fellow experimenter and we began comparing projects and notes. His name is David, and he's a southern gentleman who calls his kitchen his “lab-or-ah-tory”. I've never met someone so fearless about experimenting with food and preservation techniques. I hear that his daughters and grandson run and hide when he's ready to sample his projects!

I can relate. My husband is pretty easy going but I see apprehension on his face if I approach with a spoon and say “try this”! I'm a northern lady, and historically my people have had different issues to deal with when preserving food than David and his ancestor's in the deep south.

Our climate is cold enough to keep food outside in a cooler on the shady north-side of our house for six months of the year, and accordingly the people in the old days could hang meat in a shed or a meat house up on stilts (to keep animals out) without spoilage. In the south they had to develop ways to keep meat and other perishables from spoiling because the 'winter' they get isn't much cooler than our summers here in the north. We're far enough north in the lower-48 states that I can see the Canadian Rockies from our home up on a mountainside.

David can 'almost' see the Gulf of Mexico from his house. With modern technology, such as electric dehydrators and canners, a lot of our food preservation techniques have become the same. We've included both the new and the old in this book.

We have a couple of food preservation friends who have contributed a few things to this book. They are Pam Ritter and J D

Smith. Both could have written their own books with all the experience they have dabbling in food production and preservation. All of us are gardeners and most of us raise at least part of our own meat.

Self-sufficiency and healthy, nutritious food for ourselves and our families is our goal, and preserving those foods in a safe manner is essential.

Disclaimer! Follow all guidelines for proper food handling and safety. Wash all tools, utensils, containers, kettles, jars, dehydrator racks, smokers, and your hands before and after touching food. Process all foods for the full length recommended and store properly. Smell all food upon opening it's container and if there's any doubt, throw it out. Botulism can be deadly and food poisoned with botulism bacteria may look and smell normal. Cook meat and fish to at least 160 degrees even if it was cooked before processing. My co-writer, other contributors, and myself are not responsible for the safe processing and consumption of any food processed, preserved, or prepared by any method or information contained in this book. We've strived to give correct and safe instructions but cannot control all factors.

Section 1

Methods of Preserving

Canning

Canning is one of the most well-known methods of food preservation. There are two types of canners: Pressure canners and WaterBath canners.

Pressure canners: The pressure canner has a lid that locks down. The heat during canning causes pressure to build inside the canner, which raises the temperature inside, heating the food in the jars to several hundred degrees. The high heat kills bacteria and other pathogens. After you turn off the heat, and the food inside the jars begins to cool, this cooling creates a vacuum in the jar and sucks the lid down tight.

The rubber seal around the edge of the underside of the metal lid softens to almost-melted during the canning process, and as it cools it forms a hard, tight seal between the jar and the lid, helped by the suction created during cooling. This keeps non-sterile air from entering the jar and contaminating the food.

It is not the vacuum, or suction, inside the jar that makes the food safe to store. Otherwise we could just use a jar attachment with the Food Saver vacuum sealer to suck the air out of the jars and seal the lid. The food has to be heated hot enough to kill the bacteria, germs, and any other form of contamination, as previously mentioned. The contents of the jar become sterile. There is also probably some nutrition loss of certain heat-sensitive vitamins, but overall you are producing a safe food with many of the nutrients intact. Such things as protein and minerals aren't damaged by the canning process.

The pressure canner has a pressure escape valve with a regulator. The regulator might be a dial with numbers on it, or it might be a round metal weight with three holes for 5 lbs, 10 lbs, or 15 lbs of pressure. The amount of pressure you use during canning will determine how hot it gets inside the canner. Foods such as meat require a higher temperature, and therefore it's canned at a higher pressure.

If you live at an elevation over 1,000 feet, you'll need to increase the canning pressure by five pounds. For example, beef is canned at 10 pounds pressure at low elevations, but it's canned at 15 pounds pressure at higher elevations. I've heard it's because the boiling point is lower at higher elevations, but I would have thought the inside of a pressure canner would be a sealed environment and not affected by the atmospheric pressure outside of it. However, I stick with the recommendations even if I don't understand them, until such time I learn otherwise. You don't want to take a chance with food safety.

You can find pressure canners for sale at box or department stores, sometimes at grocery stores, and online. They range in price from around $90 and up. If you buy a used canner, check the rubber seal on the underside of the lid. See if it's dried out or cracked. You can replace it, but it's good to know upfront what extra money you might be putting out to make it usable. This is called many things, as I found on a search for places to order them: seal, sealing ring, gasket, and gasket seal.

You can order them from the manufacturer of your canner, from canning supply websites, through your local hardware store. This link will take you to canners and replacement parts on Amazon: http://www.amazon.com/s/?tag=paspr-20&link_code=wsw&_encoding=UTF-8&search-alias=aps&field-keywords=sealing+gasket+for+pressure+canner. You can find both new and used canners there, as well as the various replacement parts for different canners and other canning supplies. The same standards apply to online purchases of a used canner, however Amazon will back you if the canner is deficient and you can get a refund.

If you're looking at a used canner in person, screw the lid on the canner until it's in the locked position. See if it locks and unlocks properly. Make sure the rack is in the bottom of the kettle. It should have a slightly elevated flat rack with holes in it for water to move through. The rack is to keep the jars off the bottom surface of the canner. Placing the jars directly onto the bottom of the canner can cause them to break.

Check the small round rubber plug in the lid. It's an emergency pressure release. It would pop out if something happened to block the pressure valve from releasing steam. Sometimes the rubber has deteriorated and won't block the hole. Those, too, are easily replaced.

Lastly, check the pressure gauge. If it's the dial type you should have it tested to see if it's accurate. The county extension office can usually do this for you. If the canner has a weight with three holes on it, those don't need to be tested. When it's time to put the weight on the canner, hold it up and look for the number of pounds you need. When that number is upright, place the hole that's on the bottom of the weight over the vent spire in the center of the canner lid. When the canner reaches a pressure over the number on the weight, the weight will jiggle and release heat in the form of steam.

Make ***sure*** you have the weight when you purchase that type of canner. If it's new and in a sealed box, the weight is probably there. If you're buying a used canner make sure the weight is there. It costs $30 plus shipping to buy a new weight. If the canner is cheap enough you might find it economical to order a weight, but otherwise, be aware.

Water Bath canners: Another type of canner is called the Water Bath Canner. It probably has a proper name but that's the only one I know it by. It's a large kettle with a lid, and a basket or rack sits inside of it, for the purpose of keeping the jars from sitting right on the bottom of the canner. The jars could break if they're in direct contact with the hot bottom of the canner during the processing time.

You could use any pan or kettle that is deep enough to put the jars in on some kind of rack and still cover them with an inch of water. It doesn't have to be an official "canner". I've used a stainless steel kettle with a cooling rack in the bottom. You can use your pressure canner as a water-bath canner by covering the jars with water and not putting the lid in the locked position. Some pressure canners aren't tall enough to cover quart jars for water-bath canning, but pint and smaller jars will work.

Only fruits should be canned in a water bath process. Fruits are high in acid and don't require high-pressure and high-temperature processing to kill contaminants. Tomatoes are one of those foods that are botanically a fruit but might not be acidic enough for the water bath canner. Some people say that store-bought tomatoes are lower in acid but that if you're growing them at home, especially heirloom varieties, they have a higher acid level and are safe for water bath canning. You'll have to make that call based on your own research and belief. I would recommend pressure canning them just to be safe.

There are people who are canning vegetables and even meat with a water-bath canner, but the temperatures just don't get high enough to make me feel safe doing that. If you can't afford a pressure canner, consider using other food preservation methods, such as dehydrating, rather than risk illness or death by water-bath canning vegetables or meat.

The only things I water-bath can, besides fruits, are cheeses and butter. I'll cover those in the section on dairy products. Nuts also can be water-bath canned, among other ways of preserving nuts, which will be covered in Volume 2, to be released later this year. I only included them here to add them to the list for water-bath canning.

Canning Supplies In addition to the canner you'll need jars. You can buy new jars at most grocery, discount, and box stores. Used jars can sometimes be found at thrift or second-hand stores, and sometimes at yard sales. Occasionally they'll be advertised in the classified ads or on craigslist for sale by individuals. You can also put up a notice on a bulletin board or run your own ad asking for jars to buy. If word gets around that you're canning you might find yourself offered jars by people who no longer use them.

New jars come with one set of lids and rings. The rings, sometimes called bands, screw onto the jars after you set the lid on the jar. You can store your canned food with the rings on the jars, or take them off if you need to use them for canning other jars of food. Often used jars don't have the rings with them any more. Sometimes they bend or become otherwise unusable, so you won't have enough for all your jars. Once the lids are sealed it's not necessary to have the rings on them. If my jars might be jostled, such as when we go camping, I screw the rings on to help keep the lid from being bumped on the edge and become unsealed.

You'll need a new lid each time you can something in your jars. Reusing the lids for canning isn't safe since they are more likely to come unsealed, causing your food to spoil or get botulism, which is deadly. There is also a higher rate of jars that won't seal properly during the canning process, and then you've wasted the effort and whatever source of fuel your stove heats with.

I did try one load with pre-used lids that were in good shape, just to see how it would work. I normally have 100 % success with jars sealing, but this load had two jars out of seven that did not seal. On the shelf in the pantry, three more came unsealed in the next six months. That left two jars, and we went ahead and ate those before they, too, came unsealed.

When you use a lid on a jar for canning it leaves an imprint, or dent, in the rubber. It's possible that keeps a good seal from forming the second time, even with soaking it in hot water. There are people who reuse the lids and have success, but as long as I can buy new ones I'm not going to take the chance. I do keep the lids as we open the jars, and we're careful not to bend, dent, or mangle them when opening the jars. For now I use them on jars with dehydrated food in them, or when storing leftovers in jars. If the SHTF, either just for our family or on a bigger scale, then when my supply of new lids runs out I'll start on the used ones. At that point I would also be employing other methods of preserving food that don't require canning jars or lids.

You can buy sets of rings and lids, or you can buy just the lids. They're available at most grocery and 'box' stores. They usually come in boxes of twelve, but you can also buy lids by the "sleeve" or the case. A sleeve has 345 regular mouth or 288 wide mouth lids. A case has 60 boxes of twelve regular mouth lids, or 46 boxes of 12 wide mouth lids. Cases usually have to be ordered, either online or from a store. I order mine from Azure Standard in Oregon.

Canning lids are sometimes called "flats", "caps", or "dome caps", and possibly other names depending where you live. A regular mouth jar or lid is about 3 1/4" across, and a wide-mouth jar or lid is 4" across. I'm not sure what reasons other people have for choosing one jar over the other, but I try to save my wide mouth jars for things that are dryer or harder to get out of the jars so I can slide them right out. This would include meat like roasts, meatloaf or chicken breasts, or cheese. Other than that I just use whatever I have.

Regular mouth jars and lids tend to be cheaper to buy than wide mouth. Some people like the wide mouth for their ease in filling or emptying them, and since most people can get their hand all the way inside a wide mouth jar, washing them is easy. A regular mouth jar can be cleaned with a long-handled brush.

Other things I've heard in the wide mouth vs. regular mouth debate are that wide mouth are easier to stack, but the rims of wide mouth jars can bump each other and release the lid. Some people say that the 'shoulders' of a regular mouth jar prevents that. Food that 'floats' after canning looks better in a regular mouth jar, and leaving less 'head space' (we'll get to that) in a wide mouth jar reduces the chance that the lid won't seal.

Among other supplies for canning you'll want a funnel to set on the jar to keep the rim of the jar clean while you add the food. Funnels come in metal or plastic, wide or narrow tops. I have a metal funnel that is five inches across at the top, and a plastic one that is ten inches across at the top. The plastic one also has a removable ring on the bottom to change it from regular mouth to wide mouth. The extra-wide top makes it quick and easy to fill jars with very little mess.

A jar lifter, which looks like a set of tongs that are wide and slightly curved, is used for lifting the jars into the hot water, or lifting the hot jars out of either type of canner. They're metal and have a wooden or plastic handle on the top of each half, and are rubber coated along the bottoms so they grip the jars as you lift.

There are other 'tools' you can buy, such as one that you use to lift the lids out of the hot water that they've been simmering in while you fill the jars. It looks like a stick with a magnet on the end, and you poke it in the water and let the magnet lift the lid out of the water. I just use a fork to tip them up out of the water, then lift them with my fingers by their edges and place them on the jars.

Basie Canning Instructions Choose the food you want to can. I'll give a few examples as we talk our way through it, but there are some steps that apply to everything that is canned.

Assemble your jars, lids and rings, and assessories such as the jar lifter. Check your jars. Hold each one up and inspect for cracks or bubbles in the glass. Look closely at the rim and make sure that it is smooth, with no chips or missing pieces of glass. Run your finger gently around the rim. Set aside any with cracks, chips, or other flaws. These jars could break in the canner or the lid might not seal on a jar with chips on the rim.

These damaged jars can be used for other things. You can store leftovers in them, as well as dehydrated food, grains, pasta, herbs, or cookies. A wide mouth quart jar can hold most of a package of oreo cookies and, well, you'll just have to eat the ones that don't fit! There are non-food uses for jars that you can't use for canning. You can store buttons or other sewing supplies in them, or bolts, screws, nuts, and other small hardware, or loose change, or anything small enough to fit in the jar.

Take the jars you're going to use for canning and wash them. It's not necessary to boil or sterilize them if you're pressure canning. If you're water-bath canning and the processing (boiling) time is less than 10 minutes, you should sterilize the jars by boiling them for ten minutes and then carefully filling them with the food to be canned. It's not wrong to sterilize jars for any type of canning, but it's an unnecessary step in most cases.

Foods to be canned don't have to be 'blanched' or otherwise cooked before canning. The heat during the canning process cooks the food, so you can 'raw pack' the jars. To prepare the food to be canned it may need to be peeled, chopped, cut up, or sliced. In the case of meat you may want to brown it before canning. I find that the meat doesn't clump together during the canning process if it's browned first.

Look up the processing time for the food you're canning. If you're using a pressure canner it'll include both the length of time and the pounds of pressure. You can find the times and pressure for canning any of the foods included in this book by going to the section for that food.

Now start the lids simmering in a small pan of water. Make sure the water covers the lids and that the water isn't quite boiling. Look at the lids now and then, because sometimes air bubbles build up under them and raise them up. This can leave one side of some of the lids sticking up out of the water. Use a fork or something and poke it back under the water.

Put your canner on the stove that you plan to do your canning on. If I'm using a pressure canner and I plan to put 7 quart-sized jars in it, then I pour 2 quarts of water into the canner and start it heating. If I'm water-bath canning I fill the canning kettle about 1/3 full of water. When you set the jars in the water, the water level rises. If you've put too much water in the kettle it might run over the top by the time you add the last jar. If I need more water in order to cover the jars under at least an inch of water, I can add it after all the jars are in the water.

Take the funnel and put it in the opening of the first jar. Fill the jar with the food to be canned. You might have to use a ladle, spoon, or tongs, depending what you're canning. Allow head space. This is usually ½" to 1" and allows for expansion during the canning process. Be careful not to shove the food down and pack it in too tight. The heat needs to get all the way to the center of the jar.

For most traditional canning you'll pour water over the food unless it's a liquid that you're canning. With fruits you might be adding a sweet syrup that you've made with water and sugar, or juice. If you're canning meat you have the option of dry-canning, which will be discussed in the meat chapter.

You can add salt or sugar at this point too. I add just under a tablespoon to quart jars and a teaspoon or so to pint jars. It's not necessary, as it's not needed to preserve the food. But I figure it I'm going to add sugar or salt later when I eat the food, I might as well put some in now and have it already there. Then if times get really tough and I can't afford sugar or salt, I've already put some in when I canned.

The next step is to take a narrow rubber scraper or a knife and slide it down the inside of the jar, between the food and the glass. Do this all the way around the jar, going up and down, to release air bubbles that might be trapped under and among the food. I prefer a knife because it's easier to shove down alongside the food. Rubber scrapers can bend and get hung up on the food.

Take a damp cloth and wipe the rims of the jars. Using a fork or the handy little magnetic lifter, if you've bought one, fish the lids out of the hot water and place them on the jars. Screw the rings on as you go. Put a lid on, screw on a ring, next jar, put lid on, screw ring on, etc.

Place the jars in your canner. For water-bath canners, check the level of the water and add more if you need it. Now we're going to separate the directions.

Pressure canner: Put the lid on the canner kettle and twist until it locks. Turn up the heat if you've had the burner on low. If you're using a canner with a weight, watch for when steam starts coming out of the hole in the spindle, center of the lid. Then time it ten to fifteen minutes. As the pressure builds you might have steam escaping around the lid for a short while, especially near the handles. That should stop after a few minutes as the rubber gasket begins to seal and prevent steam from escaping.

If it keeps blowing steam out the sides, turn the canner off and remove the lid. Check the rubber gasket. If it seems dry, or if you just want to try this anyway, use some vegetable oil to moisten it. Put a few drops on it and spread it with your finger, all around both sides of it. Then put it back in it's notch in the canner lid, and put the lid back on the canner and start over, making sure to latch the lid again. Hopefully you won't have this problem, but it's usually an easy fix. Definitely try it before replacing the gasket. You might find out you don't need a new one.

This period of time is for heating the food in the jars and raising the temperature at a steady-but-slower rate than it will after the weight is placed on the canner. If you don't wait long enough you have a higher risk of jar breakage because the jars and contents will heat too quickly. If you let it go too long in the steaming stage, too much water escapes in the form of steam and your canner might boil dry before the processing time is done.

At the end of the ten to fifteen minutes of steam escaping, look at your weight. Find the number of pounds you need for the food you're canning, and set the weight on the canner with that number upright as you look at it. From this point on the temperature is rising in the canner as the steam can no longer vent out the hole and the pressure is building.

It can take a while, up to half an hour or even longer, for the pressure to build high enough to start the weight jiggling, but sometimes it's only a few minutes. When the weight starts jiggling, start timing the processing. As a quick example, green beans are canned at 10 pounds pressure for 25 minutes. Beef is canned at 10 pound for 90 minutes. This is from the time the canner reaches the necessary pressure.

The directions with my canner say it should jiggle a few times a minute. I've never been able to do that. It seems like it jiggles a bit every 10 seconds or so, and if I turn it down, ever so slowly, it stops jiggling altogether. So I settle for the more-often jiggling, as long as it's not constant or almost-constant. I've had good success with jars sealing and we've never gotten sick from home-canned food.

If you're using a pressure canner with a gauge, watch the needle as the pressure rises. If it seems to be rising too fast, turn the burner down a bit. When it gets almost to the pounds of pressure you need, turn the burner down more. If you're lucky you'll find a perfect setting that will keep the pressure about where you want it. Otherwise you might be turning the burner up and down as you go, to keep the pressure right. Try not to allow it to go more than 2 pounds above or below the desired pressure.

You have to visually babysit canners with gauges. If you don't have work to do right in the area of your canner, grab a book or a magazine and sit nearby so you can look at the gauge every few minutes. With a jiggling weight making noise on the other type of pressure canner, you can be out of sight of it but close enough to hear it and know if it's jiggling the right amount.

With both types of pressure canners, when the processing time is done, turn the heat off. DO NOT try to take the lid off at this point. Let it cool for half an hour to an hour. For weighted canners, after it's cooled for a while, take a hot pad and gently lift the weight a bit. If a bunch of steam comes rushing out, put the weight back and wait longer. Don't just leave it off and let the steam escape like that. The food in the jars will start bubbling and boiling from the sudden loss of pressure in the canner, and they can push the lids up enough to boil over and make a real mess. Then even if the jars seal, they're partially empty and you have a lot of sludge to clean out of the canner. I did this...once. Never again.

When no steam comes out the vent hole it's safe to take the lid off. You don't have to if you don't want to. There's nothing wrong with leaving everything sit until it's cool to the touch, or even go on to bed if it's nighttime and leave it all in the canner over night.
But if you're eager to see your finished product, it's safe now to remove the lid.

At this point I look to see if there are still bubbles rolling up inside the jar, or anything else to indicate that they're still really hot. If so, I let them sit in the canner for a bit longer.

Water-bath canner: Make sure your jars are covered with at least an inch of water and that they're upright, since they sometimes want to float when they're covered with water. Put the lid on the canner and turn up the heat, if it isn't already on high. When it begins to boil, start timing it. The processing time doesn't start until the water is boiling.

At the end of the processing time turn off the heat. Allow the water to cool until you can stick your finger in the water and count to ten without feeling intense pain in your finger from the heat. You can wait longer, even until the water is cold, but it's best not to take the jars out too soon.

All types of canners: Lay a towel or newspaper on the counter or table or wherever you want to set the jars. This moderates the temperature so there isn't as much of a shock to the jars as if you set them on a cold counter top or similar surface. You're less likely to have a jar break when you set it down. I'm not trying to scare you; it's very rare to have a jar break setting it down. It can happen though.

Using your jar-lifter tongs, lift the jars out of the water and place them on the towel or other surface. Leave an inch or two between them to allow air circulation for cooling. When they're cool, unscrew the rings and wash off the jars and rings. When they're dry you can put the rings back on if you want to store them that way. You can store them without the rings too.

To label the jars you can write right on the lid with a marker like a sharpie, or you can use a peel-and-stick label that you write on. Or you can use a piece of masking tape and write on that. Put the name of the food and the date you canned it.

Dehydrating

There are several ways to dehydrate food. You can buy an electric dehydrator, build a solar dehydrator, dry food on screens, use your oven on a low setting for dehydrating, etc. Some methods are a combination of drying and smoking, such as strips of fish or meat hung on poles or racks over a campfire.

The most common in America today is probably electric dehydrators. It can be hard to decide which one to buy. The first tip I would recommend is to get one with a blower in it. I've had the radiant-warmth type of dehydrator before and they don't dry evenly, even if you rotate the racks. We had a higher rate of food spoilage.

Look for one that has an adjustable temperature. Some foods, such as herbs and most vegetables, don't need as much heat as other foods, such as eggs. If you get one without an adjustable temperature, watch your first few batches of food carefully and determine if it tends to run hot. If so, you might want to shorten the drying time. It's possible to burn food in a dehydrator. I lost tomatoes, onions and strawberries in a dehydrator that ran too hot. They literally charred.

Likewise, if your food is taking longer to dehydrate, the temperature might be on the low side and you'll want to adjust your times accordingly. If your food isn't thoroughly dry it will spoil in storage. If I'm not sure, I dump the batch into a long cake pan and let it sit for a few days before I pack it to store. Our climate is very dry, so I can let it sit on a shelf, but if we're in a rainy, damp spell I set it in the oven. The pilot light keeps it warm and dry. If you don't have a pilot light you could turn the oven on for a few minutes a few times a day. That will provide enough heat and dryness for this 'curing' time.

I've burned food and melted plastic dehydrator trays in my oven because I walked away for a second and forgot to turn the oven off. I was going to count to ten and then shut off the oven, and in that short of time, I got distracted...until I smelled burning food or melting plastic. So now I keep my hand on the knob, no matter how busy I am, and count to ten, then shut the oven off.

It's not necessary to have a curing time for dehydrated foods. I just like to let the food cool from the heat of the dehydrator before I package it, and it also gives time to make sure the food really is dry. I stir it with my fingers several times a day, feeling for dampness.

When the food is dry I dump the dehydrator racks or screens into a big cake pan. Then I can pour the dried food into jars using the same funnel I use for canning, or by the handful. The other option is to pluck them from the racks with my fingers and put them in the jars. My method is faster!

In our dry climate I do a lot of dehydrating in the open air. I have some screen-type rectangular metal racks from an old dehydrator I don't have any more. I also use plastic canvas that is sold for crafts. I buy the huge size, about 18" by 24", and lay them on old oven racks for support. They make great drying racks.

Food like onions and peppers dry really well at room temperature in dry climates. I've heard you can use paper bags for air-drying leafy vegetables and herbs in humid climates but I don't understand how it works. The people who wrote me about it swear by it. They put the plants in top-first, tie the bag shut, and hang it.

If you run out of room setting trays around in your house, there are outdoor options. I've heard of people setting them in cars, with the windows cracked a tiny bit open. One year I set up a tent and used it for dehydrating. I needed to protect the food from birds and other critters, and keep the direct sun off of it.

My husband build a solar dehydrator that we used for several years. It had a tall, narrow box for the top part, with drawers that slid into the box. The bottoms of the drawers were screens, so when the drawers were inside the box, air could move upward through all the drawers and out through a screened vent at the top of the box. The screen was to keep bugs out and allow heat to escape.

At the bottom of the box, on the opposite side from the screen, he built an angled surface going down to the ground. He ran a board down the edge of each side and it looked like a slide going down from a small playhouse. He put a piece of metal roofing on the 'slide' and painted it black. Then he laid a sheet of glass across the tops of the edge boards creating an airspace above the black metal. There was an opening at the bottom for air to come in, and at the top it opened into the box with the screened drawers.

The black metal heated up and the the heat rose under the glass and up into the box. It worked good for things that didn't need a lot of heat, or that wouldn't spoil over night while the sun was down. I dehydrated a lot of peas and blueberries in there over the years. We had excesses of them and it gave me a handy place to dry them while I dehydrated other food in the house.

My current electric dehydrator is a Nesco dehydrator from Wal-mart. It has a temperature control, and I can order extra trays for it. It does the best job of dehydrating tricky foods, like eggs, of any dehydrator I've used.

David:

My first dehydrator(s) were the inexpensive "Oster" models from Wal-mart. I had two of them and bought them about seven years ago, and although they were single temperature "Blow and Go" models, there were workhorses and very dependable. I still have an use them on occasion. Limitations: They only had four trays that tended to break easily and replacements were expensive. Only a single temperature (about 150 degrees) and would tend to cook some foods.

The second type that I had was from Wally's also. I bought it a couple years ago and it was a newer "Oster" model. It, too, was a single temperature, "Blow and Go" type. The trays were larger and made of better plastic, but the first one I bought didn't work right out of the box and it's replacement died after about 20 hours of intermittent use.

The one I have now, I ordered from "Pleasant Hill Grain", a Nesco-American Harvestor 1018. It has adjustable temps from 95 to 160 degrees, trays that are 1 square foot, expandable to 30 trays. I have 38 trays and sometimes use them all, despite the recommendations. The airflow is good and it is almost impossible to block off the air. It also has temperature cut-off to prevent overheating and fire.

It's a workhorse and I put it through it's paces for about six months, then had to have it repaired. It then lasted about another six months and finally died. The amount of food it dehydrated was probably far more than it was designed for though. I did have some issues with the service department at Nesco, but as frustrated as I got with them, I still think Nesco's are good machines.

Freezing

If you have a large freezer or adequate space in the freezer part of your refrigerator, freezing food can be an efficient way to store food. When we lived in town and had 'grid' electricity we had a large upright freezer. It was handy to have, especially at harvest time when I was already busy, or when something went on sale really cheap at the grocery store.

We live off-grid now and have enough solar electricity to power a 10-cf frost-free fridge and freezer combo from spring to fall. The freezer holds about as much as a microwave oven, to give you an idea of the size. Not big, but not tiny like a dorm-room fridge. I make use of it when my raspberries are ripe. During the peak of the crop I get one to two gallons of raspberries a day, depending how good the berries are doing in general in a given year.

I freeze the berries temporarily in bags until I have enough for a canner load. I also do this with fish. I freeze the day's catch after we've been fishing, and when I have enough I thaw them, pack them in jars, and run them through the canner.

The main concern, especially from a 'prepper' point of view, is that if the power goes off, you have a lot of food that could spoil. Most people know that during a short-term power outage they can keep the door of the freezer closed and everything will stay frozen for a couple days.

You can also cover the freezer with all the extra blankets, sleeping bags, or rugs that you can find, to help insulate it while the power is off. Unplug it from the wall until the power is back on, or better yet, turn off the breakers or main power for the house to avoid surges when the power comes back on.

Some people have bought or plan to buy a generator and gas/diesel to power it. If you hook it into your house wiring set-up, be SURE you have turned off the power that goes to the grid so you don't electrocute a lineman working on restoring power. They can be many miles away and still be killed.

A generator is only useful, in my opinion, for a short time period. It's a pain to keep putting fuel in them and running them. It doesn't sound bad, to start it up a few times a day and run it for an hour at a time, and it's a reasonable option for most people. But with everything else going on it can get to be a wearisome chore, according to some of the experiences people have recounted after hurricanes and other disasters.

It's *not* a good option as a long-term solution for a wide-spread event. I wouldn't recommend storing huge amounts of fuel and planning to use a generator for months or years. For one thing, if a situation that bad happens and everyone is out of power, the noise of your generator will attract attention. It's like a dinner bell.

Don't believe that your generator is quiet and won't be heard. I've had people tell me that. People who live in civilization are used to the background hum of utilities and motors. Even when there are power outages there are still motors running, electronics such as battery-powered radios, music players, cell phones, and gasoline-powered generators, chainsaws, and other tools being operated.

Here in the wilds of Montana, in an area that is sparsely populated and largely off-grid, I can hear a neighbor's generator 3 miles away. I can hear a chainsaw more than 5 miles away. If we get into a long-term situation I would not want to be operating anything with a gas-powered motor after everyone else was out of fuel.

If you have reason to believe the power will be out for a long period of time it's a good idea to get started right away on preserving the food. Some things like vegetables could be spread on trays, cookie sheets, even bed sheets spread on the floor, and dried. If you have a woodstove or an outdoor campfire you can thin-slice meat and make jerky.

Canning is an option if you have the jars and a way to heat the canner. Some gas cookstoves will still work when the power is out, but many have electronic lighters for the burners. Some of these stoves have automatic gas shut-offs for when the power goes out, but some can be lit by hand with a lighter or match. If yours has pilot lights you can still use the stove and oven.

You can use a canner on a campstove, but they can be hard to fit on some of the smaller campstoves. It is possible to use a canner over a campfire but it's hard to keep the temperature hot enough. A water-bath canner is more successful since it's not hard to keep water boiling over a campfire.

Obviously the little alcohol stoves some preppers keep with their emergency supplies wouldn't do the job of canning. They are, however, still useful to keep on hand for emergency cooking.

If the weather is cold enough you could move some of the food to coolers and set them outside. Put them out of the sun, and cover them if you can. Select the foods most likely to be okay if they thaw slightly. The newer information I've read is that meat can be refrozen under certain conditions.

The meat should have been kept cold, meaning not having been left to sit at room temperature at all. It should have been in a sealed bag or other container the entire time it was in a thawing state; the reason being that the meat is protected from bacterial or other contamination during that time. It should only be refrozen once.

If this happened to me and I had to refreeze meat, when the power came back on I would work on canning that meat, or I would cook it and then repack and freeze it. That way I would not have to worry about another power outtage and losing that particular meat by having it thaw again. Be sure to mark the packages of any meat that has thawed or partially-thawed and been refrozen, and use them up first.

The supplies for freezing food are very simple. You need a container to put the food in. It can be a bag or plastic boxes. These things come in 'freezer' varieties, and as much as possible, you should use ones that are labeled for 'freezer'. Other bags and containers might not protect the food from freezer burn. If the food to be frozen doesn't have a high water content you can use glass jars to freeze them. Expansion of liquids would break glass jars as it freezes.

Freezer burn is what happens when food loses moisture and dries out. It happens when air reaches the food while it's frozen, and it's not always because there's a hole in the bag or a lid came loose. Thin plastic bags seem airtight but air does permeate the plastic and the oxidation dries the food. If you have no choice but to use these bags, double-bag them. Freezer-burned food is still safe to consume but the texture and taste might not be pleasing.

Vacuum-sealing your food is a good way to extend it's life in the freezer. The bags that are used with vacuum-sealers are already heavy enough for freezer use, and sucking the air out with the vacuum sealer keeps the food from oxidizing. It doesn't insulate to help keep the food cold, it just seals it in an oxygen-free environment. It'll keep for twice as long as stored in traditional bags, and can be used for all types of frozen food.

The vacuum sealers are running from around $50 and up, at the time of this writing, winter 2012-2013. There are attachments you can buy that will vacuum-seal glass jars, and some of the pricier units come with the attachments. If you're using a lot of bags it can get expensive.

Weigh your options. If your freezer isn't very big or if you're good about rotating your frozen food and using it in a timely manner, say less than six months from the time you froze it, you might prefer to use regular freezer bags.

Another option is freezer paper. The food is wrapped in plastic as thin as saran wrap and then wrapped in the freezer paper. It's generally white or brown paper, similar to the paper that paper sacks are made of, and it comes in rolls like aluminum foil or wax paper. After you wrap the food you tape it with freezer tape or masking tape.

My research has come up with conflicting opinions about whether you should pack your freezer tightly, or arrange things to allow for air flow. Our freezer has a blower at the back, so we leave air routes to allow circulation. I don't know if the food to the front of the freezer would stay as cold otherwise.

I've always heard that if your freezer or refrigerator are more than half empty, you could cut energy costs by putting jugs of water in there. When the water becomes cold or frozen, it helps maintain the temperature in the unit. Water expands when frozen, so pick your container carefully.

One-gallon size plastic milk jugs work pretty good. Leave a couple inches of airspace at the top to allow for expansion and the cap unscrewed so the air can escape as the water freezes and expands. Once it's frozen screw the cap on tightly. Sometimes these jugs crack, so if the power goes off or you take the jug out of the freezer, be careful where you set it. You might have water running all over as it thaws. Sometimes the cracks are hard to see.

Some of the half-gallon jugs that you can buy drinking water in are made of a heavier plastic and have concave bottoms, which makes them a better container for freezing water. You can also put bags of beans or rice in a freezer for cold thermal mass.

Freezing stops the activity of enzymes, bacteria, and other microbes that spoil food, but it *does not kill them!* When the food is thawed, they resume activity. This means the food will spoil if you leave it at room temperature, so be sure to cook and use it right away, or dehydrate, can, or otherwise preserve it.

This means that raw meat that has been frozen and thawed has the same dangers as raw meat that has never been frozen. Use care in handling and wash your hands thoroughly afterward. Do this even if you touch frozen raw meat.

Make sure the food you are going to freeze has been prepared and ready for freezing. This could be peeling, cutting, slicing, and/or cutting up the food item. Some foods need to be "blanched", cooked, or browned before canning.

Blanched means to bring water to a boil and then dip the food to be canned in the boiling water. I use a metal strainer basket with a metal handle on each side. I find a pan big enough to accommodate the strainer and fill the pan with water. I put the pan on the stove and turn up the heat. The food to be frozen goes in the strainer. Sometimes it takes more than one strainer load to do it all.

If you're going to freeze large amounts of food that need to be blanched, now and in the future, you might want to invest in a two-part pot designed for this purpose. The inner pot has holes like a strainer all around it, and you set it inside the outer pot after it boils. You can blanch a lot more food at one time.

The food stays in the boiling water for anywhere from 1 to 10 minutes, then you remove it and run cold water over it to stop the cooking process. The purpose for blanching is to kill off the enzymes that cause food to decay, or 'rot'. Freezing doesn't stop the enzymes on vegetables and they'll keep working away at destroying your food.

Blanching time is in accordance to the density of the food. Denser food needs to be blanched longer. These times will be given for each food in their own section, and fruits and vegetables will bc in Volume Two, so you'll have to wait for it's release later in 2013.

Be sure any food that you put in the freezer has thoroughly cooled. Fruits and vegetables can be cooled at room temperature. Meat can be cooled in the refrigerator before freezing. This is usually leftovers from a meal.

My mother had a stand that she could clip a bag into. It came with something called a “Seal-a-meal”, which was a predecessor to the vacuum-sealer. The seal-a-meal sealed the top of plastic bags closed using a heated press, but did not suck the air out of the bag. The most useful accessory was the stand, though. Once the bag was clipped in, you put a funnel in the top, and you could ladle food into the bag without mess, and without holding the bag while you fillcd it. We often used the stand for ziplock freezer bags.

A quick internet search came up with several 'Bag holders' but none that looked like my Mom's. None of the ones pictured showed anyone using a funnel to fill the bags. In fact, one picture showed someone pouring right from a pan into the bag. My hand isn't that steady. I use a wide funnel to reduce having messes to clean up.

Brining and Salting

This is one of the oldest ways of preserving food. Brining and salting are both 'salt' methods of curing food, Long ago the availability of salt could make the difference between life and death.

I've never done any salt curing, but my co-writer, David, does a lot of it. He served some salt-cured meat to us on a visit to his house this fall, and other than tasting salty it was delicious. It can be rinsed and be less salty, but this was sliced right off a chunk of salt-cured meat with no washing.

My husband owns a few older books on meat preserving and I read through those, plus did internet searches. I've also picked the brains of a couple of other people I know who do or have done this type of curing. The information I'm sharing is technically only theory to me since I haven't done what I'm about to share with you.

The difference between brining and salting is that in brining you are soaking meat in a solution of salt, which may or may not include seasonings as well. When you 'salt' cure meat you rub the salt into the meat.

There is a lot of variation to methods and lengths of time, both for curing and for storing. From what I've learned the meat can sit for months in the brine solution, but should be kept cool.

It's not exactly a long-term storage method, but it would still be useful. For example, if you have salt but no canning jars, you could preserve food long enough that you could eat it up before it went bad. In the case of a long-term power outtage it would be an easy way to preserve some or all of the meat in your freezer. “Long term”, to me, means longer than a week or two, but it can also mean permanently.

The brining mixture is something most of my sources agree on. Keep adding salt to water until a fresh egg will float on the water. What if you don't have a fresh egg? The best I could come up with was a website that recommended 6 tablespoons of salt to 2 quarts of water. That doesn't seem like enough to me. If I had a fresh egg I'd measure the salt as I added it, to find out what I get. I also found a site that recommended 1 cup salt to 4 cups water, and another site that said “add salt to water in a pan that is simmering over low heat, until the salt will no longer dissolve. Then it's salty enough”.

Being a native of the cold north is probably why I don't know much about brining or salting. It's not an effective way of curing when the weather is cold, strangely enough. Temperatures below 34 keep the salt from penetrating to the center of the meat and curing it. People in our part of the country historically used the cold temperatures of winter to preserve meat.

Meat was usually hunted or butchered in the Fall and eaten before it got too warm in the spring. Over the summer, which is short in the north, meat was generally from small animals such as chickens, rabbits, or fish, and it was butchered or acquired as it was needed, so there was no need for preservation.

My southern friend, David, comes from the part of the country where curing meat was the norm back before refrigeration. It's still done but more for flavor than for preservation. You can buy curing mixes at most grocery stores, sold near where the salt is, and there are probably recipes and measurements on the box or bag.

Most table salt is iodized, and salt with iodine in it can't be used for brining or salt-curing. Be sure to buy non-iodized salt. Sometimes it's labeled as 'pickling salt'. If you're going to do a lot of salting, or if you're a 'prepper' and want to buy large amounts of salt to store, Costco and Sam's Club sells non-iodized salt in 25-lb. Bags. Right now

(December 2012) it's around $4 a bag, which is pretty cheap for a bag that size. It's a cheap item for preppers to store a lot of, for your own use and as a barter/trade item.

To make a brine you mix the salt and water, add spices and seasonings if you wish, and put the meat in it. Your dish or container for brining can be plastic or glass, but not metal. There would be a chemical reaction between the solution and the metal that could cause off-flavors or make the brine funky.

If your meat floats in your container and is exposed to the air above the brine, you can weight it down with a clean rock. When I asked David, my co-author, he told me he uses a canning jar full of water as a weight. If you're brining a large piece of meat or any piece of meat with the bone in it, you can use a basting syringe to inject brine between the meat and bones, as well as injecting the brine deep inside the meat. This will help ensure that the meat is cured all the way through.

Salting the meat is done by rubbing the salt into the meat, pushing it into crevices and up along bones. Then it's left to sit, sometimes just open to the air, sitting on papers. Most of the directions I read said to salt it a second time after a week. You can mix spices and herbs with the salt when you rub it on the meat. The spices and herbs were originally used to repel insects as the meat cured. Early people liked the flavor it gave the meat, which led to all the different combinations of seasonings you can buy now.

Some people hung the meat for a couple weeks after it was cured, and then smoked it. It's not necessary to do one just because you did the other.

Meat can be packed in barrels with layers of salt above, around, and below it. That's how meat was preserved for the wagon trains that crossed the United States in the 1800s. Beef or pork were layered with salt in a barrel and strapped to the side of the wagons. Occasionally it would go bad, but for the most part it kept the pioneers fed on their journeys. It was also done for sea voyages. Many of the methods of food preserving were 'invented' as ways to keep sailors fed over long months at sea.

In conversations I've had with friends while working on this book I've gathered that one reason people don't salt-cure meat these days is the whole health issue of high blood pressure and excess salt intake. Modern methods of meat preservation, such as canning and freezing, have done away with the need to salt-cure meat, and those methods produce a food with a much lower sodium content.

Meat isn't the only thing that can be preserved by salting. Vegetables such as green beans can be brined. Instructions for those will be given in the vegetable section under 'green beans', along with all the other ways you can preserve green beans, in Volume Two.

It's a good thing to know how to salt- and brine-cure meat and other foods, in case we lose the ability to use some of the modern methods. No matter how much you prepare and how many supplies you store, someday you might not have the jars or canning lids to can meat, or the electricity to power your freezer.

I asked David how he stores the meat after the brine- or salt-cure is done: *"I tie cords/strings to the pieces of meat and hang them from hooks on the front of the shelves where I store some of my jars of food. Then I tie a cotton pillow case around them to keep away any bugs or other "critters" that may try to get after them.*

Hanging them keeps any moisture that may be left in the meat from condensing between the meat and shelf that it may be sitting on. It is important that the cured meats be allowed to "breathe" if they have any real moisture left in them.

I have wrapped the cuts in waxed paper, then put them in cloth bags and put them on the shelves. That works okay (so far) for meats that are dried to almost zero moisture. But if they are that dry, they can go into a sealed bucket. I have stored some that say too.

My plan from now on is to hang the cured meats with a bag around them. That is how my great-grandparents did it. I remember seeing hams hanging in their kitchen, inside bags. They would usually leave the meats in the smokehouse through the winter and only bring it inside when they needed it. That's how they would store it, once inside."

Sugaring

Sugaring is much like salting, only the ratio of sugar-to-salt is much higher. For example, David's sugared roast beef calls for 4 to 5 cups of sugar and ½ to 1 cup of salt. Those directions are in the meat section of this book. Sugaring has also been used to preserve fruit, vegetables, and dairy products in some cultures. There is a great recipe for "Dolce de Leche" in the milk section, contributed by David.

Smoking

There are two kinds of smoking: hot and cold. Hot smoking is generally done with temperatures above 85 to 90 degrees, and can be done as hot as 225 degrees. Cold smoking, obviously, is using smoke and temperatures less than that, usually 70 degrees or less.

Hot smoking is the kind most often used with commercial smokers and sometimes crosses over to what is called "barbeque". It's mostly a way to slow-cook meat with smoke and heat. It's great for breaking down the fibers of tough meat like brisket. Hot smoking doesn't penetrate all the way into the meat and isn't technically a food preservative. It can, however, produce some mighty tasty meat. The heat dries out the surface of the meat and creates a barrier, which prevents the smoke from penetrating deep into the meat. With cold smoking the outside of the meat stays soft and the smoke penetrates all the way to the center of the meat, killing bacteria as it dries the meat.

Cold smoking is often done in the winter unless you live in the far north where summers are cool (and sometimes downright cold!). In the old-time smokehouses where cold smoking took place, they often started the fire in the morning and let it smolder all day, then started it again the next day. Cold smoking is done in cycles, rather than steady like hot smoking.

With hot smoking you want to keep the smoke moving around all sides of the meat, all the time. The wood of hickory, oak, apple, and mesquite are among the most popular used for smoking. Keep the chips piled tightly as they burn to reduce exposure to oxygen so that they will just smolder and produce smoke. Otherwise they'll burst into flames, which isn't want you want for smoking.

You can use a barrel for a smoker, or make a pit, or buy a commercial smoker. You can find commercial smokers from around $50 up to several hundred dollars. If you're not sure smoking is something you'll want to do a lot of, buy a cheaper one and if you go nuts with it, look into getting a better one. One of my son-in-laws has a cheap smoker and is really into smoking meat and fish. He does it quite well, too. I imagine he has a bigger and better smoker on his wish list!

Hot-smokers usually have the fire in the same containment space as the meat, whereas cold-smokers usually have a separate chamber for the fire, and the smoke goes through a tube or pipe into the chamber where the meat is.

If you are wanting to learn to smoke meat as a form of preservation I suggest doing cold-smoking since the finished product has a shelf life of several months and even years. For preppers, this is the way to go, especially if you have a limited amount of canning jars and supplies. In addition to meat and fish, you can also smoke cheeses and nuts.

Meat and fish are soaked in a brine solution overnight. You can add seasoning and flavor like a marinade if you want, but smoking by itself gives meat a great taste. Although most modern meat-smoking is done for flavor rather than preserving, the smoke will seal the meat and prevent oxygen from reaching the meat, thereby slowing down the growth of bacteria and other scientific and microscopic creatures. This gives it a much longer life in the refrigerator and freezer than raw unsmoked meat.

The shelf life of cold-smoked meat is determined by the combination of salt/brining and dehydrating that take place along with the cold smoke working it's way through the meat. For meat you plan to store I'd use a strong salt mixture for your soak, around one cup salt to one cup water. Don't cut your smoking days short. Give it a good long time to absorb the smoke and dry out.

Remember, if you started with raw meat, you still have raw meat. It still need to be cooked when you're ready to eat it. Be careful handling it and wash your hands thoroughly before and after touching it. Even if you use pre-cooked meat for smoking, good hand-washing practices help keep bacteria *off* the meat as well as off of and out of you.

The bottom line for me is that I would soak the meat in a strong brine solution, at least overnight and probably for a few days. I would cold-smoke the meat for several days to make sure it's thoroughly dried and the smoke has time to penetrate through the meat, which means longer for bigger cuts or hams, and shorter for smaller cuts. I would then store the meat in a cool, dry place. Depending on the time of year that might be outside in one of our sheds, in vacuum-sealed bags to prevent oxygen exposure and in a barrel to protect it from critters and moisture; or I would store it the same way in our root cellar, protected from oxygen, rodents, and moisture, and where it's cool and dark.

If I couldn't meet all of those conditions I would freeze or refrigerate the smoked meat and try to use it within a few months. If the power goes out you could build a quick smoker in your backyard (if you have a backyard. I always hear from apartment dwellers pointing out they don't *have* a backyard. You can't just use any yard-type area or commons or park, unless you have people to help watch over it at all times) and start smoking the meat. I'm talking about if the power goes out and you don't expect it back on any time soon. First determine which type of smoker will work for your current weather. If it's hot summer weather, then you should hot-smoke the meat since you won't be able to cool the smoke enough for cold smoking.

If, for some reason, you don't have water to spare for a brine you can salt the meat instead. Rub salt into the meat, including into cracks, under flaps, in along bones, until it's completely covered. In a few hours you might want to turn it over and salt it again. Use non-iodized salt for both a rub and for a brine.

Get your meat, cheese, or other food soaking in the brine or salted while you build the smoker and cut wood. You'll need a hatchet or an ax to chop the wood into chips. The type of wood in a disaster/emergency situation isn't as important since you're just trying to save the meat from spoiling and not as worried about gourmet flavor. It should be hardwood though. If you have to use softwoods like Pine I'd shoot more for the heat-and-dehydrating preservation rather than smoking, per se.

If you have to dig a pit to smoke your meat, make your fire in the bottom of the pit. Keep it smoky. Once you have the fire going add 'green' wood chips to make smoke. Remove the meat from the salt solution and rinse it off. Suspend the meat over the smoke on sticks, or find a rack such as an oven rack and put it right on the ground over the hole and set the meat on it. The smoke should keep away insects, but you may have trouble with dogs, cats, or other critters. Assign someone to attend the fire/smoke and guard the meat.

The meat will still need to be kept cool when done smoking or drying, so wrap it and cover it with newspapers or blankets or anything insulating to keep it as cool as possible, and make it a priority to eat it soon. If you have a rodent-proof container you can bury it to help keep it cool. Set something over where you've buried it to keep the sunshine from heating the ground at that spot, assuming you are getting sunshine. A cool basement or root cellar is also a good place if you have access to one.

From David: "*I haven't smoked that much meat, but there are a few things to watch. First, you want to remember to only use good quality wood that hasn't been treated with any chemicals. What you burn is what you will wind up eating. Pines and other evergreens usually have quite a lot of sap that will not leave a very good taste in the food. Most hardwoods are okay. Second, like a dehydrator, you want to make sure you don't let the temperature get too high and allow the meat or other food to cook. You want a cool smoke to dehydrate, and not to cook.*

Meats that have a lot of fat will smoke and dry okay, but will take longer and the fats may tend to go rancid over time. The fats going rancid does not mean that the meat is bad, just that it may not taste as good. Try to choose leaner meats to smoke.

Pickling and Fermenting

These are actually two completely different food preservation processes. Pickling is preservation by using a fermented product, vinegar. Before you can pickle, you have to ferment something into vinegar. Vinegar can be made from anything that contains sugar, but is most commonly made with apples (apple cider vinegar) or corn (white vinegar). It's an ancient process that can be done at home, but since you're not able to control or measure the acidity it's recommended that you don't use it for food preservation. You can, however, use it for fresh things, like on salads, or for household cleaning.

Vinegar is a fermentation process using a sweet liquid such as fruit juice, and the type of yeast used in wine-making and beer-making. It's not brewer's yeast or bread-making yeast. They're mixed and left to sit for a few weeks at about 60 to 80 degrees. At cooler temperatures fermentation might not take place; at warmer temperatures it might spoil.

Picking is the use of the vinegar to preserve food. It imparts a unique flavor in addition to preserving. Vinegar can be used alone, or you can add mustard seeds, dill seeds, or follow a recipe, depending what you're pickling. Just about any food can be pickled: fruits, vegetables, meat, eggs, and probably a lot of things I've never heard of. If you can put it in a jar and cover it with vinegar, it can probably be pickled, and someone has probably tried it.

Some recipes call for canning the pickled food after you cover it with vinegar. Other people are horrified at the thought, since canning (and freezing) will kill the 'good' bacteria but not necessarily the bad bacteria in the vinegar. That's a call you'll have to make yourself.

From my co-author and side-kick, David: "*With pickling, the big thing you need to watch for is to make sure that your jars, crocks, and utensils are sterile and that you have thoroughly washed the food to be pickled. Some germs/yeasts can live in high-acid and high-salt environments and you don't want to cultivate them (usually).*

If you are brining foods to ferment, you want to make sure that you don't use too much salt. If too much is used, you will wind up preserving the food in salt and not allowing it to ferment. After the 'pickles' have finished fermenting, it will be necessary to "freshen" them to remove enough salt to make them edible. Sometimes it is not necessary if the salt was carefully measured when the fermenting was started. Be sure and taste the food to make sure the salt content is okay before you seal them in jars. Do not double-dip your spoon and introduce germs/bacteria into your pickles."

Ash, Oil, and Honey

Ash: David came across information in an old book on meat preservation about using ash in preserving meat. The book only had one sentence just stating that meat can be covered with ashes. Since then he and I, as well as a few friends other preppers, have been discussing and debating how it worked. Some of our friends thought maybe the meat was already cured and was just buried in ash to protect it from mice and insects. Others had a theory that the ash would draw out liquid, which would dry the meat and 'cure' it, and some went further to suggest the liquid would mix with the ash and create lye, which could also work to preserve the meat. In that case, a person would want to use ashes from hardwood rather than pine, since softwoods don't create lye when mixed with water. If the meat was already cured, the ash could work like sawdust to keep air, as well as pests, off of the meat, but would still allow the cured meat to 'breathe'. Despite extensive internet searching none of us were able to find out more, and all the old-timers we could ask don't remember such a thing.

Oil in either solid or liquid form has been used at different times throughout the world as a preservative. Food of all kinds could be coated with oil or put in a crock to soak in it. Lard or other solid fats were sometimes melted and poured over food, one layer at a time, and then the container covered. Some of these worked better than others, and I would use them only as a last resort.

Honey is anti-bacterial and has been, and still is, used as a preservative. The meat or other food was layered with honey in a crock, then covered, the same way oil or lard was/is used. It creates a barrier between the food and contaminants. It's still used in Egypt and the middle east. The honey should be raw, unpasteurized honey.

Some words from David

Big spending is not a requirement for getting into food preservation. Most of my "equipment is inexpensive standard-type kitchen items. I use 'Granite Ware' Pans for cooking large batches of foods to be canned, for blanching foods, for brining and curing, and as 'Water-bath Canners'. I use enameled pans so that food acids and lime (for making hominy) will not damage them. The granite ware also works well for soap-making. Lye will eat up most non-enameled cookware. I try to make sure that every item has multiple uses. It cuts down on storage space requirements too. I also use quite a few plastic kitchen basins. They make good working containers when I process foods, for everything from temporary storage to brining. They are cheap, hold a lot of food, and are easy to pick up at just about any store.

Wrap up

This concludes the first part of this book, the descriptions of food preservation methods and the tools needed to do them. Now we move on to the second part of this book where I have listed each food and what methods of preservation can be used with it. I've also included directions on how to prepare, process, and store each food with those methods. I'm sure there are many more that I've missed, or small variations that other people do, but this is based on my own experiences and those of the other contributors to this book. Any additional information we get after this book is published, in the form of comments, reviews, or emails, will be on the blog that was listed in the introduction to this book.

Section 2

How to preserve each food

Meat

Beef, Venison, and Elk

I've lumped these three together because they're often used interchangeably and they're processed or cured the same way. For those unfamiliar, beef is from cattle, venison is from deer, and elk is from elk. Don't assume everyone knows that. We had a man visit our homestead from New York City in 2005 and when we mentioned that hamburgers and beef came from those cows in the field, he got mad and thought it was was a joke country people played on city people and that we were making fun of him. He went home a week later still not believing the beef on the supermarket shelf came from cows, and he's a smart man, a computer geek/techie. I'm serious.

I'll refer to all of these meats as 'beef' as I write this section.

Canning: Pressure canning is the only safe procedure for canning beef or any meat. Water-bath canning isn't considered safe for these types of foods because they are low-acid foods and the temperature in a water-bath canner doesn't get high enough to kill all the pathogens and bacteria. Please don't take a chance on sickening or killing anyone by water-bath canning meat.

Meat can be prepared several different ways for canning. You can grind the meat and can it as ground meat or make it into hamburger patties and can them. Steaks and roasts can be canned but they won't be the same texture as fresh steaks and roasts. Stew chunks are pieces of meat cut into 1" to 2" pieces.

There are two main ways to can meat: traditional canning, where you cover the meat with water or broth; and dry-canning, where you process the jars of meat without adding liquid. You must be careful with dry-canning meat. If the meat is dense, like a roast or ground meat crammed into a quart jar, the heat might not get high enough in the center of the meat to kill all the pathogens. Do not pack the jar tightly with dense meat.

When we process a cow, deer, or elk, we trim off as much fat as possible to give the finished product the longest shelf-life possible. Fat becomes rancid faster than lean meat. Even if you buy meat at the store, look for the leanest meat or trim the fat yourself. Some meat such as venison develop funny flavors if the fat is left on them.

Processing time and pressure for Beef, Venison, and Elk:

Quarts:
90 minutes at 10 lbs pressure if you're less than 1,000' elevation
90 minutes at 15 lbs pressure if you're over 1,000' elevation.
Pints:
70 minutes at 10 lbs pressure if you're under 1,000' elevation
70 minutes at 15 lbs pressure if you're over 1,000' elevation

Here are the ways I prep and process meat for canning:
Roasts: I cut them to the size where they'll fit easily into a wide-mouth jar. The reason I use a wide-mouth jar for these is so that they'll slide right out of the jar without getting hung up in the neck of a regular-mouth jar. Sometimes I roll the roasts in a mixture of flour, salt, and pepper, then brown them before putting them in the jar. I've also just put a raw chunk of meat into the jar and canned it just like that. It's not necessary to cook the meat first since the canning process will cook it.

I add about half an inch of water to the jar, but you can fill the jar with water or broth to about an inch from the top, leaving 'head space', if you want to can the traditional way. It does make for a moist and juicy roast, and you'll have 'broth' in the jar by the time the roast is cooked. Follow the procedures for putting on lids, etc., from the canning directions in that section of this book. It'll become like second nature and you won't have to look them up each time.

Steaks or chunks: Steaks can be sliced until they're of a size that will fit into a jar. You can also cut the meat into chunks that can be used for things like stew, stir-fry, or pot pies. Chunks can also be shredded by hand after canning and mixed with barbeque sauce for some excellent "pulled beef" or barbequed beef/venison/elk. Browning is optional. These do quite well with the traditional cover-with-water method, keeping the meat nice and moist. If you dry-can it and the meat seems dry when you open the jar, soak it in luke-warm water for a few minutes.

Ground meat: You can pack the jars with ground meat that you want to use later for chili, spaghetti, tacos, sloppy joes, or whatever you use ground meat for. If you're going to cover the meat with water I recommend browning it first. It won't be quite as watery when you open the jar and use the meat. It takes a lot of frying to boil all the water out of it when you use it. I prefer to dry-can ground meat. I brown it first, then crumble it into the jar. When it's browned before canning it crumbles apart better when you open the jar to cook a meal with it. For this I use regular mouth jars because digging or spooning the meat out of the opening of the jar doesn't damage the meat like trying to pull a roast or burger patty through a smaller opening.

Hamburger Patties: I form hamburgers patties, using a wide-mouth jar lid as a pattern. One of the readers of my blog suggested using the wide-mouth jar ring like a cookie cutter instead, and that's a great idea. Next time I can patties I'm going to try that. The reason I use a pattern is so that the patties aren't too big to put in the jar, and not so small that I waste space in the jar.

When the patties are formed I brown them in a frying pan, then remove them to a plate to cool. I stack them in wide-mouth jars, four in a pint, eight in a quart. The number you fit in the jars might depend on how thick your burgers are. I use wide-mouth jars so I can slide the burgers out of the jar when I open it. If they seem 'sticky', run a knife around the inside of the jar, then slide the burgers out. Gently peel them apart or run a knife between them to separate them. Handle with care so they don't crumble apart. Place them in a pan to heat them, or put them in the microwave.

David told me that he doesn't brown his patties. He cuts waxed paper to fit in the jar, then layers raw patties with the paper so he can get them apart after canning.

Prepared meat: I have canned meatloaf by mixing the ingredients with the meat and packing it into a wide-mouth jar, either pint or quart. To remove the canned meatloaf, slide a knife around the inside of the jar, and/or dip the jar in hot water, before sliding the meatloaf out of the jar. Meatloaf is tricky. The texture is better if you dry-can it, but you must be sure not to pack it too densely so that the heat gets all the way into the center of it.

You can mix herbs and spices with the hamburger meat before you can it, to give it a mexican or italian flavor, or other types of flavor. I've browned meat chunks in ginger, garlic, and soy sauce (as well as oil) and canned them for stir-frys. You could experiment with marinades for roasts, steaks, or chunks. I have been told by some that the meat should be canned plain, and that it can ruin the flavor by running the herbs and spices through the canning process. I haven't had that happen with anything I've canned, but keep it in mind and decide for yourself whether you like how your meat is coming out.

Dehydrating: Most people think of jerky when they think of dried meat. Jerky is easy to make, and there are dozens of ways of seasoning it. But meat can also just be dried just as chunks and steaks. Cooked hamburger meat can be spread on trays and dried. Use the warmest temperature setting on your dehydrator if it's variable.

If you're starting with raw meat cut it into pieces about 1/4" thick. Cut with the grain, not across it, so the pieces won't shred or come apart after they're dry. The meat will shrink considerably as it dries, so don't cut your meat into too thin of slices.

This is where a good marinade can be handy. Cover the meat slices with the marinade of your choice and set it in the refrigerator for a day before drying the meat. You can also spread the meat in the dehydrator and sprinkle it with seasonings instead of marinading it.

In the old days a lot of meat was dried near or over an outdoor fire. This sometimes crosses over to smoking meat, but is considered drying. You can do this by slicing the meat into thin slices and putting it on racks near the heat of a fire, or hanging it over poles placed over or near the fire. There has to be enough steady heat to dry the meat without letting it spoil. Usually the smoke from the fire will keep most of the flies and other insects off of the meat.

Whichever way you dry the meat, be sure that it is indeed dry and ready to store. Vacuum-sealing it can extend it's shelf-life, as will storing it in a cool, dry place. Plan on using it within 6 months.

Freezing: This is about the easiest and fastest way to preserve meat. The way we did it was go wrap the meat in white freezer paper and tape the packages shut with a freezer tape that looked something like masking tape. Sometimes we wrapped the meat in saran wrap first, then in the freezer paper. We wrote on the paper with a marker, describing what type and cut of meat it was, and putting the date on it.

Nowdays you can seal the meat in the heavy vacuum-sealed bags and freeze it. There isn't any prep work required. Just take your meat cuts or ground meat and wrap or seal it, then freeze. Raw, unfrozen hamburger patties will stick together if stacked, so spread them out on greased cookie sheets or wax paper-lined sheets or trays and freeze them. Once they're frozen you can stack them in a bag or other container and put them back in the freezer. They won't stick together that way. As you thaw them, separate the burgers as soon as you can.

Brining and Salting:

This is an excellent way to preserve meat, if you have access to a lot of salt. It can take 10 lbs of salt to cure the meat from a cow, and 5 lbs for a deer. If you're planning ahead for it right now, you can buy 25-lb bags at Costco, and probably at Sam's Club too. Some grocery stores sell 5-lb boxes of pickling salt, which is coarser than table salt but works just as well. Be sure to go back to the section on brining and salting in the how-to in the first part of this book for more specific directions.

Sugaring:

Here is David's information on sugar-curing beef:

Sugar-curing beef is similar to salting/brining except that the preservative is sugar-based instead of salt-based. If you have ever eaten a country ham or beef jerky you know that it can be too salty to eat a large enough quantity to satisfy your dietary needs without planned preparation.

With sugar-cured meats the salt content is largely replaced by sugar, and can be sliced and eaten directly off the slab without overloading your system with salt, and risking nausea, dehydration, or worse.

Select a mostly fat-free roast about 2 inches thick and of a size that easily fits into your container without bending or rolling it. Some fat it okay, light marbling is good but trim off any excess or pieces not firmly attached to the roast. I prefer rump roast or round roasts, about 2 to 2 ½ pounds in weight. They have about the right amount of marbling and easily fit into my containers. The recipe below is for a cut that is 2 – 3 pounds.

How to Sugar-Cure Beef

In a 3-gallon or larger pot, measure in about 1 ½ gallons of water and add 4 – 5 cups sugar and ½ to 1 cup salt. I use regular table sugar and coarse rock salt. The rock salt is cheaper than table salt and I have quantities of it stored for food preservation. A general rule for the curing solution is that it should be strong enough to "float and egg".

Bring the liquid to a boil and ensure that all the salt and sugar dissolves, then let it cool to a temperature that will allow you to put your hand into it without scalding or discomfort.

Place the roast into the solution. It will try to 'float' and will need to be weighed down. Canning jars full of water work well to keep the meat down below the water level.

If the roast floats or any part rises above the liquid it could spoil or attract insects. Cover the pot and keep it in a cool-to-cold place until the cure "strikes through" the cut of meat.

The cure usually takes at least two full days to 'strike. You can recognize that it is done when you can remove the cut and it will hold it's shape and appears darker in color. It's better to stay too long in the cure than to be taken out before it's done.

When the roast is removed, rinse it in clean water and allow it to air-dry to the point that water does not drip from it when it is held in the air. It should still be damp and tacky enough to hold a coat of salt.

Place it in a container on a bed of table salt and make sure salt completely coats it, then leave it to air dry. Turn the cut several times a day so it will dry evenly.

To speed the drying, I put a small fan blowing over the container to help evaporate the liquid drawn out by the salt. As the meat dries you may notice the bed of salt it is laying on becoming damp. No worries, the liquid that doesn't evaporate into the air will be drawn into the bed and evaporate from there.

Drying will take about 7 – 10 days in a good cool, dry area. When the meat can be pinched between your fingers and no moisture surfaces, it is done. The roast should hold it's shape when held horizontally by one end.

With a sharp knife, slice a thin piece off one end to check the color and texture. The inside should be a dark red to brown color and be very dense, and any fat marbling should be solid and the color of shortening. Any loose or ragged pieces of meat or fat should be trimmed off, and any salt/cure should be brushed off with a vegetable brush.

Some old recipes say to dip the cured meat into a pan of boiling water for about a minute to remove any crusted salt and/or 'cure', and to kill any germs that may be present, then left in the open air to dry before storage.

Some of the old procedures for storage call for the pieces to be wrapped in fresh, clean paper and placed in a muslin bag and kept in a cool, dry location until needed. It is said that meats preserved in this manner can remain good for up to five years or more.

Personally I'd shoot for one year, to be safe. I have pieces wrapped in paper, covered with a cotton pillow case, and hung from hooks on a shelf to promote air flow and to help keep pests away. I also have pieces vacuum-sealed and they seem to be doing well after about 3 – 4 months, so far. I'm not sure if the cured cuts need to breathe yet, or if vacuum-sealing is a better option, but the experiment is still ongoing. If you visit our blog there will be updates on my experiments with preservation: http://www.povertyprepping.blogspot.com

Smoking Meat:

Other than ribs and brisket beef is not smoked as often as other meats, such as hams and fish. However, it can be done. If you're smoking it for long-term storage, use the cold-smoke method. It'll take days or even weeks, but if you build a good smoke-house or smoking barrel, you only have to start the fire once a day and let it smolder. Although hot-smoking is considerably faster, you do have to stick around and keep the fire fed, or should I say, keep the *smoke* fed, since you don't want it to burst into flames and burn up your chips. Hot-smoking doesn't thoroughly cure and preserve the meat, so you have to have a way to keep the meat cold and eat it sooner than with cold smoking.

Cold-smoked meat can be stored for months. Trim as much fat off the meat as you can to prevent it going rancid. Be pretty surgical about this and get as much off as you can. Mix a saline solution of 1 cup water to 1 cup salt. Add spices and flavorings such as you would use to marinade the same cut of meat, if you wish to add flavor. Let it sit overnight. Some people say put it in the refrigerator, others say it only needs to be a cool place. If you get too much below 30 or above 50 the salt won't absorb properly, so try to keep it in that range.

Remove the meat from the brine solution the next day, pat it dry, and take it to your smoker. Place it on the shelf or rack, hang it from a nail or hook, or spear it on a stick, or however you intent to place it during the smoking process. Follow the directions in the 'Smoking" section of this book, depending whether you're hot-smoking or cold-smoking, or the directions for your recipe if you're using one.

Hot-smoked meat should be refrigerated or frozen. It will keep in the refrigerator for a few months, and in the freezer for a year; longer if wrapped properly. Cold-smoked meat, if started with a strong salt solution and then dried well during a long smoking process, should keep for months even on a shelf. You can set it on newspapers and cover it with cloth, or put it in a cloth bag and hang it. Keeping it in a cool and dark room will extend it's edible life.

Pickling:

Meat can be pickled by cutting the meat into small pieces, about 2" in size. Store the meat in the refrigerator or a cool place while you prepare the pickling liquid. The liquid can be just vinegar, or you can add other things such as mustard seed. You'll need about a pint of vinegar for each pound of boneless chopped meat. Use a total of a quarter cup of seed or seasonings.

Put the vinegar and seasonings in a pan and bring to a boil. Let it boil for 3 minutes, then put in in a jar and screw the lid on tight. Put it in a cool place or in the refrigerator. After the liquid cools, add the meat and stir to remove any air bubbles. Screw the lid on tight and put it back in the cool place or refrigerator. Allow to sit for a few days before eating it. It'll keep like this for about a year, sometimes longer. Watch for discoloration or swelling. This could indicate that it's gone bad.

Oil-Preserving meat:

(David) *"A way to preserve cooked meats without canning or freezing is to store them cooked and covered in lard. I have heard this being referred to as "Potting Meat".* (Commercial Potted Meat is a canned product of parts of the animal you probably don't want to know about !) *I gave it a try last year with ground sausage patties, ham slices, and bacon (ends and pieces). It would probably work well with any cooked meat or poultry but I haven't tried it with anything but pork yet.*

The process calls for a crock jar to be used to store the meat in but I didn't have that much meat to work with, so I used one-gallon pickle jars instead. The only think I was concerned about was the jar cracking when the hot lard was poured in, but that didn't happen. The person I first heard from about how to pot meat used a well-made wooden box with a lid that was nailed on the top when the box was stored for the winter. His family did this during the depression, so they used whatever container was available.

Heat a pot of lard to around 300 degrees. The exact temperature is not critical but should be hot enough to kill any germs it comes into contact with, but not so hot that it starts to smoke.

Cook the meat to be stored completely. No pink or rare to medium-rare shoulid be used. Right out of the pan, place some of the meat in a layer on the bottom of the container and pour a layer of the hot lard over it. All pieces should be completely covered. Repeat until you run out of meat or until the container is full. The last layer on top should be lard, and it should be deep enough that no meat shows through. The last layer of lard will act as a barrier to bacteria and everything else, and preserve anything under it.

Put the lid on, or cover the container so that no "critters" can get in. Some processes that I have read call for an oiled or greased cloth to be tied around the top of the container. When the container is cool enough, store in a cool place until needed.

When needed, take pieces from the topmost layer, being careful not to disturb any deeper layers. If no more of the contents are going to be needed for a while, pour another layer of hot lard over the top to reseal it.

To prepare the potted meat, just heat it enough to allow any excess fat to drip off and drain from the pieces. This method of preserving meat is meant to keep it over the winter and not through the heat of summer, so don't plan to use this procedure to store meat in the long-term. The lard may become rancid in warmer weather.

Pork and Bear

I've put these two meats together because they're quite similar and can be processed and preserved the same. Bear meat makes great sausage. The rest of the bear we use as roasts and chops. With pork you can also make hams and bacon. Pork comes from hogs or pigs, and I know many of you are rolling your eyes and saying you knew that. However there may be people reading this who didn't. I have met people, *adult* people, who didn't know.

Canning:

Like beef and other meat, pork must be pressure canned. Water-bath canning isn't considered safe for these types of foods because the temperature doesn't get high enough to kill all the pathogens. Please don't take a chance on sickening or killing anyone by water-bath canning meat.

Processing time and pressure for Pork and Bear:

Quarts:
90 minutes at 10 lbs pressure if you're less than 1,000' elevation
90 minutes at 15 lbs pressure if you're over 1,000' elevation.
Pints:
70 minutes at 10 lbs pressure if you're under 1,000' elevation
70 minutes at 15 lbs pressure if you're over 1,000' elevation

Pork chops can be canned but keep in mind that they will be fragile when you lift them out of the jar. The meat falls apart easily and although you'll have the flavor, you won't have the texture. Pork roast is excellent for canning. The fats in the roast cook through the meat and you end up with a very tasty, moist piece of meat. You can drain the liquid off when you open the jar and make an awesome pan of gravy with it. Then you can serve the roast on the side, or break it into pieces and mix it in the gravy.

Roasts or chops can be cut into chunks or slices and canned for stews or stir-frys. I like to season mine with ginger, garlic, salt, and pepper and then can them for asian cooking. Some people can them with chopped snow peas, peppers, and water chestnuts, then add them to Asian noodles when they later cook a meal with it.

Ham can be chopped, sliced, or shredded, then pack into jars and canned. It can be used in ham salad sandwiches, grilled ham and cheese sandwiches, omelettes, as a topper on baked potatoes along with shredded cheese, on pizza, in bean soup, and many more ways.

Bacon can also be canned. Lay a piece of was paper on a table or counter, then lay the uncooked bacon strips on the wax paper, Put another piece of wax paper over it, then start at one end and roll it up tightly. It might be too tall for your jar and there are two ways you can handle this. Some people fold the wax paper roll in half and put it in the jar. A wide-mouth jar would be the best option. I cut the bacon strips in half, thus making a shorter roll.

We make pizza/Italian sausage and breakfast sausage with ground pork or bear. I brown the Italian sausage and can it in pint or half-pint jars. It can be a regular-mouth jar since you'll be spooning the meat out and don't need to worry about a wide opening. With breakfast sausage I crumble and brown some of it, then can it like the pizza sausage for use in biscuits and sausage gravy, or to add to things like chili or lasagne. The rest of it is made into sausage patties, browned, cooled, then stacked in jars for canning. I don't worry as much about size on these as I do hamburger patties, since these are usually on the side of the plate next to eggs or biscuits, rather than placed on a bun. With hamburger patties I want it to more or less fit the bun. So making smaller sausage patties is okay.

Ground pork can be canned plain and used however you would use fresh pork. It's often mixed with ground venison to add fat to the venison. Straight venison is very lean and it's hard to get hamburger patties to stay together.

We've canned hot dogs and they swelled up and split. I haven't done it since I started dry-canning meat, so maybe it would come out better without being submerged in water.

If you've butchered the hog or bear yourself you can save and render the lard. Cut the lard into chunks one to two inches in size, then start melting them down in a kettle over very low heat. You don't want it to get hot enough to smoke. After it's in a liquid state pour it through cheesecloth or something similar to remove bits of hair or other 'stuff'. Pour it into jars and screw the lids on. They'll seal as they cool and it'll keep this way. As with all fats, store it in a dark, cool place. Light is the enemy of fats and oils.

Dehydrating

I'm reluctant to write directions for this because if pork isn't dried under the exact right conditions there is a big risk of bacterial infestation such as botulism. The bacteria thrives deep in sausages and hams, and even with a salt/brine soak the dangerous pathogens can survive. A lot of people prefer to avoid nitrates when possible, but if you're going to dry pork, you should use sodium nitrate ("pink salt"). There is something else you can add that creates a fermentation process that produces lactic acid, similar to how yogurt is made. I've never dried pork, and although I could rewrite what I've read while researching this, there are too many variables and too many things that can go wrong. Find specific directions from a reliable source if you want to do this.

Freezing

Pork chops, roasts, breakfast sausage, and bacon can all be frozen, thawed, and used with little change from using fresh pork. Hams can be frozen, both uncooked and cooked, but should be wrapped carefully. Vacuum-sealing is best, but a plastic and paper wrap is good too. When poorly packaged during freezing it can change the fibers of the ham and the texture can be altered. Some people don't notice the difference, others notice it so much they won't eat a ham that has been frozen. Ham releases quite a bit of water during thawing, so be sure to set it in a bowl or other container if your ham isn't packaged in something water-tight. To extend the quality of all pork to be frozen, go the extra mile in packaging it well before freezing. Remember, edible doesn't always mean culinarily delightful.

Brining/Salting

Brining and salting are classic methods for preserving pork. It can be done with a brine solution, by rubbing salt onto the pork, or by layering the pork with salt in a barrel, and sometimes a brine solution is poured over the pork and salt in the barrel. The specifics for brining and salting are in the section on those methods, but I'll include David's information on curing pork layered with salt:

"Cut the pork into strips crosswise against the grain. Cutting the fibers makes it easier for the salt to be absorbed into the pork. The meat should be cool but not cold. Cover the bottom of a clean barrel with salt, then pack in the strips of pork, tightly, edgewise with the rind next to the barrel. Fill the crevices in between with salt, and cover the top of the layer of meat with more salt. Proceed in this way until all fo the pork is in the barrel or until the barrel is filled. Make a strong brine of salt and cold water, enough salt that an egg with float. Boil and skim the bring, then pour it over the pork in the barrel while it is boiling hot. Cover the pork with a piece of board, then put a rock, jar of water, or other weight heavy enough to hold the pork down in the brine. Cover the barrel and leave it in a cool dry place. If at any time the brine should froth or look red it should be poured out, scalded and skimmed, and poured back over the meat again. Never put cold bring

on old pork. We have done this for years and never lost any. When you want to use the pork, freshen it by letting it stand in warm water in a warm place for about half an hour.

Bacon and hams are made or cured with salt. That's what gives it that delicious salty flavor. One of my favorite ways to do bacon is after it's been salted a couple times, we rub it with pepper for another day.

David usually brine-cures hams, and I asked him how long they would keep: "*A well-cured ham or bacon should keep at least a year to 18 months, and per "Blob" (friend's screen name), he said that he has kept hams for up to 5 years without problems. I don't really think they will last that long down here though, because they'd be eaten before that much time goes by! When I was stationed in Italy there was an account of a farmer that found a 100-year old Prosciutto in his store house and it was still edible and tasted good.*

I got a fresh wild hog shoulder from my brother-in-law today and I have it curing in the outside fridge right now. I used a basting syringe to inject the cure deep into the meat next to the bone, to speed up the curing time. Since I have it in a cold fridge I am going to let it cure for at least a week before I take it out."

That was on December 5th. On December 7 he wrote: "*I took out the hog shoulder I have brining, to check on it today. It's been in about 2 days, and by the feel and look of it, it will be ready to take out of the liquid in a few more days. I did this one a little different. I mixed a quart of boiled-down cranberry syrup in with the brine, thinking that would be an interesting touch, maybe hide some of the gaminess of the wild hog. It was a fairly plump hog and I cut off all the skin/rind and only have the bare shoulder soaking. My brother-in-law soaked the hog in a cooler of salt water before I got it, to leech out some of the blood, but I didn't figure that into the brining time since the shoulder still looked pretty fresh when I got it.*

On December 18th he wrote: "*I took the hog shoulder out of the salt basin tonight, brushed off the salt, and sliced off a piece to sample. It didn't taste much like a store-bought ham, more like proscuitto, but it was pretty good. With the sugar cure it wasn't too salty to eat like a country ham, but some salt did migrate in from the basin it was drying in. I'm going to let it dry a little more, then I'm going to store it like the Italians do with their prosciutto's. I'm going to smear a light coat of lard over the outside to keep it from drying further, then hang it from a shelf without a cover over it.*

But...the plot took some twists: "*I changed my mind a few times on how I was going to store it. I thought about just hanging it then decided that I didn't want it to dry out completely like some of the other meats I have hanging, have dried out. Several times I put the piece of shoulder in a food-saver bag and sealed it to see if the vacuum would draw out any more moisture. It did, several times, so I put it back into the salt to dry some more.*

I settled on the vacuum-sealing to store the shoulder and it seems to be doing okay. This piece of meat is going to be an ongoing test. Every month or so I am going to open the bag and check on the quality. I'll do this until about mid-summer so I can see if it will survive the summer heat without going rancid or spoiling.

If you'd like to know how that goes, we'll have regular updates on the blog: http://www.povertyprepping.blogspot.com. We'll label those posts "David's Kitchen – Hog shoulder experiment", then number the updates so you'll know when a new segment is posted.

From another good southern friend and fellow prepper, JD Smith, I got this great recipe for curing meat:

½ cup kosher salt
½ cup maple sugar
½ to 1 teaspoon cloves

Mix and rub into meat. You can use this for bacon or ham. I don't use sodium nitrite. Put the meat into a plastic container for four to seven days for bacon. If it's bacon, flip it ones a day. If it's ham it will take two to three weeks, for five pounds of meat. Again, I don't use sodium nitrite but if you want to, put in one tablespoon.

One thing I want to add to this is that any time you use maple sugar or maple syrup it has to be the real thing. Imitation maple flavoring changes flavor and tastes weird in the finished product. Don't scrimp on this. If you can't afford maple sugar or maple syrup, use brown sugar. It won't produce a maple-cured flavor but it'll stay true to the taste of brown sugar, which is also pleasant.

After bacon is cured you can store it as it is, or smoke it. Smoking isn't used on it's own for curing bacon because it only affects the outer part of the bacon. It's used for flavor. Store bacon in the refrigerator or freezer. It can be canned, too. In the United States bacon is usually cut in strips, while in Europe it's mostly available as cubes.

Smoking:

Pork meat lends itself well to smoking. Interestingly, the worst, lowest grade cuts are the best for smoking. The tough, grisly fibers break down into a tender product during the long, slow process of smoking. Good lean cuts of pork can dry out, so save those for other types of curing, such as canning or salting/brining, and use the almost-inedible cuts for smoking. A brisket, for example, can become a mouth-watering barbeque.

You can also smoke hams and bacon. For those I'd use the hot-smoke method since you're mostly flavoring them, rather than preserving them. You can do the brisket this way but it you want truly tender meat, use the cold-smoke method with brisket. Follow the directions in the smoking section for both methods.

Pickling:

Nothing on a pig went to waste in the old days. When all the meat had been made into roasts, chops, hams, sausage, and bacon, they made cheese out of the head, used the intestines for sausage casings, and pickled the feet and "hocks" (basically the ankles). They fried the ears and dried them to make snack food, rendered the lard to use as shortening/grease/fat, and fried up the cracklings, which are bits of meat filtered out of the lard, and which make a tasty treat.

Any part of the pig/hog can be pickled. This sentence made me wonder what the difference is between a pig and a hog. A quick google search came up with this: A pig is a young swine weighing less than 120 lbs (50 kilograms), and a hog is an older swine weighing more than 120 lbs. I'll probably keep using them interchangeably, and I hope you go with me on that one. The meat is processed the same for both.

To pickle pork, follow the directions in the pickling section, doing a brine or marinade soak first, then making the vinegar/pickling solution and putting the meat in jars with the pickling liquid poured over it.

Headcheese is actually a meat product and not a cheese. It's a jelling and pickling of the head, and I've never found myself inquisitive enough about it to make it. If times of starvation came along we'd probably be making it from any and all of the animals we processed. When I lived in a rural part of SE Kentucky I talked to people who had eaten a lot of things the rest of us think we'd never try. They had to, to survive during and after the depression. One tidbit of advice left a lasting impression on me. A woman advised me that groundhog should be eaten very hot, or else it will taste greasy. I've heard the same thing about porcupine. Groundhog seems appropriate in the pork chapter.

Goats & Sheep

A lot of people have trouble thinking of these as meat animals. In peace time and when things are economically going well in prosperous nations like the United States, there aren't that many people eating goat meat, and although sheep meat is more commonly eaten, it's way behind beef, pork, or poultry. The meat is edible, but since most foods are a learned taste and often cultural, it might take some getting used to.

You know how people joke about "It tastes like chicken"? Well, neither goat or sheep taste like chicken. I'd say goat tastes more like squirrel, or like turkey drumsticks. Really, it doesn't matter. For most people it's the idea of it that is the biggest obstacle to overcome. You can marinade the meat in seasonings and cook it, and you'd have a hard time distinguishing it from other similar meat.

Seventy-five percent of the word's population eats goat meat and the demand for it is fast-growing in the United States. Among dairy animals world-wide, more goats are found than cows. This is partly because dairy goats require less space and less feed, and they're easier to manage. They're also cheaper to buy and make a nice addition to a small family farm or homestead.

If you have dairy goats you have to breed them annually so that the goat will continue to produce milk after the birth of the baby. If the baby is female it's often kept to help build the herd, or sold as a dairy animal. The males are raised and butchered for meat, or sold to someone else for meat. We had an adorable little billy goat given to us a few years ago. We took it to clear brush around the edge of our yard where the woods started. That worked well. We put a dog collar on him and put him on a runner chain and moved him around between trees.

All went well for the first year. We never really had a long-term plan for him. My husband talked about using him for a pack goat when we go backpacking. As he reached his first birthday he became temperamental. He was big and strong, and he head-butted us a few times. Finally my husband began talking about goat meat. I thought he was joking. He wasn't.

A goat is a lot like a deer when you butcher them. Once it was skinned, it was easy to stop thinking of him as a goat. I had that "oh no! Ick! It's *goat* meat!" thing going, but I steeled myself because I know goat meat is edible and it wouldn't make me (phsically) sick. I've done the same when we tried muskrat once. We ran a muskrat trapline for a couple years and a do-gooder lady thought that was terrible, even though the muskrats had over populated the marshy area alongside the lake near us and they were fighting over food. She said it was disgusting to kill an animal we didn't eat, so.... we did. And posted pictures on our blog! It actually tasted better than goat, though being mixed into a kettle of muskrat and dumplings with lots of onions, celery, carrots, and potatoes was a little different than slicing off bites of goat roast. Despite the seasonings on the goat roast, it was still meat by itself.

Goat meat is called 'Chevron' if it's from an adult goat, and 'Cabrito' if it's from a kid/yougster (think...veal).

Sheep meat, or mutton, is often eaten at Easter time in the spring. You've probably heard of Leg of Lamb, often served with mint jelly. Meat from an older sheep will have a stronger flavor, which probably explains the preference for lamb over mutton. I haven't eaten mutton or lamb in quite a few years, so I barely remember it. My mother served it occasionally, and I don't recall it being objectionable.

I looked up recipes for lamb with mint jelly and there were so many

I couldn't decide which one to share here. Everyone has different tastes. I know my Mom basted the lamb with oil mixed with salt and pepper. She put some of the mint jelly on it but I don't remember if she did it early on during the baking, or toward the end. She made the mint jelly by boiling apples, mint leaves, sugar and …? I don't know the rest. Why am I wasting *your* time by putting partial information in here? Probably sentiment on my part. My Mom died in 2004. I miss her.

Canning, Dehydrating, Freezing, Brining/saling, Smoking, and Pickling are all possible with goat and sheep meat. Follow the directions for beef.

Rabbit

In my opinion rabbits are the ultimate meat animal for the individual or family. They're prolific, meaning they reproduce on a large scale. They don't take much space, they're quiet, and they don't smell bad. The manure is among the best you can use for composting for a garden, to improve the soil. And one of the biggest reasons, they're easy to feed. You can grow things for them, including a patch of alfalfa. You can forage for them, gathering branches from willow trees and shrubs. You can feed them all sorts of scraps from fruits, vegetables, and grains. You can even feed them the stuff you trim off or peel off vegetables and fruits as you process them. They like carrot tops, turnip tops, and all other tops, and apple peels, potato peels, the pods from peas as you shell them, the husks from corn on the cob, and more. You can rake the lawn when you mow and throw it all in to your rabbits, as long as you haven't sprayed anything on the lawn If you find yourself unable to buy rabbit feed, odds are you can keep your rabbits fed.

Domestic rabbit meat really does taste like chicken, but it's sort of like the thigh meat. It's not really dark meat and it's not really white meat. The entire rabbit is all 'medium', like chicken thighs. You can use it in place of chicken in all recipes. There are recipes created just for rabbit, such as the famous German dish, Hasenpfeffer, which is rabbit stew, more or less.

Canning:

Rabbit must be pressure canned, like all meats. You can process it at chunks, roasts, or ground rabbit to use like hamburger meat. I've never tried to make rabbitburger patties so I don't know if they will stay together and formed. Rabbit tends to be lean meat, and lean meat is more likely to crumble apart when you try to press or pat them into patties. Rabbit can be packed into jars raw or cooked. Some directions call for soaking the meat in saltwater before canning. I canned rabbit for years before I heard of this. I add a tablespoon of salt to each quart when I can rabbit or any meat.

Processing time and pressure for Rabbit:

Quarts:
90 minutes at 10 lbs pressure if you're less than 1,000' elevation
90 minutes at 15 lbs pressure if you're over 1,000' elevation.
Pints:
70 minutes at 10 lbs pressure if you're under 1,000' elevation
70 minutes at 15 lbs pressure if you're over 1,000' elevation

Dehydrating:

Since rabbit meat is so lean, it is a good candidate for drying and makes good jerky. Season it like you would beef or venison jerky. Another good way to dehydrate rabbit is to grind it, cook it, and dry the crumbles. It's leanness gives it a longer shelf life than fattier meats, and if you vacuum-seal it and store it in a cool, dry place, it'll last even longer. We assume about a 3-month shelf life but we've eaten it as long as a year later. The key is the cold, dark, airt-tight or vacuum-sealed storage. Heat, light, and oxygen are the enemy of all dried foods.

Freezing:

Rabbit meat can be frozen the same way as beef, chicken, or any meat. Package it well, in vacuum-sealed bags, in doubled plastic bags, or in plastic and then paper wrapping. There are also plastic freezer containers you can use, if your meat will fit into them. Rabbit can be frozen with the bones or deboned, raw or cooked.

Salting or Brining:

This can successfully be done with rabbit, and is actually a good way to preserve it because you can add flavor with seasonings in the brine or marinade. Follow the directions in the section on Salting and Brining. Again, the lean nature of the meat lends itself well to this and most types of preservation and curing, which is another "plus" for raising rabbits for meat.

Smoking:

You can smoke rabbit meat but because it's a fine, lean meat you have to be careful not to over-dry it. The meat will be stringy, hard, and tasteless. Rabbit meat is pretty bland, smoking does impart a nice flavor to the meat. Cold-smoking will be less likely to dry out the meat as hot-smoking, but watch the meat carefully and check I periodically.

Pickling:

Rabbit can be pickled like any meat, and is actually common in some places. There's also a version of Hasenpfeffer where the meat is soaked overnight in vinegar and salt, then breaded and fried the next day. That isn't a true preservation method, but sounds tasty anyway. Follow the general pickling directions in that section of this book.

Chicken

Chicken is a versatile meat and can be cooked and preserved in more ways than just about any other food.

Canning:

Chicken can be cut apart at the joints and canned as pieces with the bones intact, or but from the bones. You can cook it, let it cool a short while, then debone and can it. Or you can grind the meat and can it as ground chicken. The meat has to be raw for grinding, but then you can cook it and then pack the jars, or raw-pack the ground meat into the jars and process it.

My favorite way to can chicken 'chunks' is to boil the chickens in a huge kettle, then use tongs to lift them to a strainer basket. When it's cooled enough to touch I go through and pull the meat from the bones with my fingers. I fill jars with the pieces of meat, then ladle broth from the kettle I boiled the chickens in, and cover the meat in the jars. Leave 1" of headspace, which is the air space at the top of the jars. I put a teaspoon of salt in a pint and a scant tablespoon in a quart.

Processing time and pressure for chicken:

Quarts:
70 minutes at 10 lbs pressure if you're less than 1,000' elevation
70 minutes at 15 lbs pressure if you're over 1,000' elevation.
Pints:
50 minutes at 10 lbs pressure if you're under 1,000' elevation
50 minutes at 15 lbs pressure if you're over 1,000' elevation

Dehydrating:

There is a lot of difference in recommended ways of dehydrating chicken. It's a lean meat and will dry quickly, and although it has a good flavor on it's own, it takes well to a wide variety of seasonings and marinades. Chicken should be cooked before dehydrating and should be dried at a hotter temperature than non-meat foods. A minimum temperature of 140 degrees should be used for dehydrating chicken.

Pressure cooked chicken, including canned chicken, works best for dehydrating. Just cooking the chicken and then drying it can leave the meat stringy and brittle. By using chicken that has gone through the pressure cooking process first, you'll end up with a dry meat that isn't tough.

Cut the cooked chicken into ¼" strips or chunks. Soak in marinade for about 2 hours, if you're using a marinade. You can dry-season the meat if you'd rather, or dry it as plain chicken. Cooked chicken that is then dried at 140 degrees should take about 5 or 6 hours. To reconstitute it add warm water or broth to the meat and allow to soak until soft, about ½ to 1 hour.

Freezing:

Raw and cooked chicken can be frozen to preserve it. Wrap in plastic and then in paper, or vacuum-seal it, or double-bag it. It can be frozen on the bone or deboned, as well as ground. The better you wrap it, the longer it will keep.

Brining and Salting

These can be done to chicken as easily as any other meat. Again, it's already a somewhat dry and lean meat, so watch that you don't over-do it.

What follows here is a series of emails I received from David as he brined a chicken. The first one is from December 7: "*I put a whole store-bought chicken in brine today. I used the basting syringe and injected as much brine as the bird would take, in the wings, legs, thighs, back, and breast, and made sure that brine was in the later between the skin and meat. I then put it in the pot and poured the remaining liquid over it. I put a glass plate over it to keep it down, and put a quart-sized jar of water on top of the plate to keep it down. I put the lid on the pot and put it in the outside fridge.*

By the feel of the chicken it's going to take a while to brine. The legs and wings seem to be just about firm enough but the breast is still soft, so I'm letting it go back into the fridge to soak longer. I haven't decided how to dry it yet. I may put it in a bin of salt and do it like I have been doing the beef and pork, or I may hang it in the cardboard tube dehydrator and try it that way. I think I still have about two or so days to decide.

I tried a chicken about a year ago but just packed it in salt and let it sit for about a month... one of the failures I don't mention! I wound up just dumping it over the fence. Curing and drying poultry really has me concerned about the safety, but my friend, who goes by 'old coot', says he does it successfully, so I thought I'd try it his way. I have no idea how it will come out, but will keep you informed."

December 14: "*The chicken seems to be doing okay. It has a way to go to dry to the point that I would feel good trying to store it. The wings and legs seem to be drying faster than the rest, so I may just trim them off, cook them up, and see how they come out. If I survive, I guess I can give my stamp of approval. At this point, I can't see much advantage to curing them as long as I can pressure can it, but in the future it may be useful. If a large quantity could be cured and hung in a smokehouse to dry, it may be worth doing."*

December 30th: "*The jury is really still out, with the cured/dried chicken. I took it out of the salt this afternoon and it doesn't really look very appetizing. I wound up making cuts in the skin and into the meat to speed the drying, which makes it look pretty ragged. It seems the skin is pretty effective in keeping moisture in. The fat content in and under the skin make the color kind or yellow, but it's dry and doesn't have an offensive smell. It does kind of smell like "wet chicken" though."*

January 5: *"I cooked the cured/dried chicken and just took it out of the oven. I pulled a small piece off the breast and tasted it. It was a bit salty but edible, and it's texture was like reheated baked chicken, kinda dry.*

To prepare it, I first soaked it in warm water for an hour and changed the water, then boiled it twice for about 15 minutes, each time with fresh water. Next, I rubbed it with oil and baked it in a covered cast iron pot for 60 minutes at 350 degrees."

Later on January 5th: *"The chicken was just too dry and still too salty after being boiled twice and then baked, so I brought out the small pressure cooker and pitched it in for 45 minutes. After that it was pretty good. The funny thing is that alrhough it had been pressured at between 10 and 15 lbs (that's what the small cooker cooks at) it was still pretty dry. It is my opinion that chicken, and likely any other poultry, that is salt cured and dried is best stewed and not prepared any other way. The stock was pretty salty also but diluted down it will make a decent soup.*

Curing poultry would not be my first choice in preserving, but based on the experiment, I would say that it is do-able, and since I didn't suffer any ill effects, it is likely safe."

Smoking:

Chicken comes out great smoked but it dries out easily and the skin can get rubbery. It's best to use a brine or marinade rather than just rubbing salt into the meat. Coat it with oil when you're ready to smoke it, or push dabs of butter inside the skin.

Pickling:

Pickling chicken is mostly a use-now sort of thing, such as using pickle juice for a marinade, however pickled chicken can be preserved for storage too. Follow the directions in the pickling section of this book, using whichever pickling method you choose. There are even such delicacies as pickled chicken feet, gizzards, and hearts, and I even found directions for pickled fried chicken, to which I could only wonder....why? :)

Turkey

Turkey is delicious all year round, even though in the United States it associated with Thanksgiving. That is a good time to find good prices on turkey, and a good time to stock up and preserve it for eating later in the year. If you have a place to raise them they're fun to raise. Ours follow us around like puppies. People are often nervous about raising turkeys, thinking they're delicate, disease-prone, and “so dumb they'd drown staring up into the rain with their mouths open”, but we've never had any problems with ours, other than them persistently being underfoot when they free-range. Commercial turkey meat is less likely to be raised in confinement and given antibiotics or other drugs. They tend to be raised commercially in large fields rather than in cages.

Canning:

Turkey, like all meat, must be pressure canned. It is not safe to water-bath can turkey because the temperature doesn't get high enough to kill all the pathogens and bacteria. Please don't take a chance on sickening or killing anyone by water-bath canning turkey.

To can turkey: cook the turkey, then debone it and put the meat in jars. If I've boiled the turkey I use the broth to fill the jars around the meat, if I'm canning it the traditional way. Turkey meat is on the dry side, so I don't usually dry-can turkey meat. When I roast the turkey in the oven and I plan on canning it I make sure to keep water in the bottom of the roasting pan, adding it as needed. After the turkey is cooked and I remove it from the roasting pan I use the water in the jars with the meat. I spoon it evenly into all jars, then add hot water to finish filling the jars. That way I have an even amount of the 'drippings' to flavor each jar. I add a teaspoon of salt per pint and a scant Tablespoon of salt per quart. Salt is optional, as are other seasonings you might like to add.

Processing time and pressure for turkey:

Quarts:
70 minutes at 10 lbs pressure if you're less than 1,000' elevation
70 minutes at 15 lbs pressure if you're over 1,000' elevation.
Pints:
50 minutes at 10 lbs pressure if you're under 1,000' elevation
50 minutes at 15 lbs pressure if you're over 1,000' elevation

Dehydrating:

Turkey Jerky is a great treat. You can even use leftover turkey meat for this. Slice either raw or cooked turkey into thin strips. Cut with the grain so the strips won't fall apart when they're done and you lift them up. Stir together salt and seasonings and mix with water, then submerge the meat in the marinade (seasoned water) and refrigerate over night. If refrigeration isn't available use more salt in the marinade and set it in the coolest place available.

The reason I don't give measurements is because it varies depending how much meat you use, and how salty or spicy you like your jerky. My favorite is to put tablespoon or so of salt in the bowl, about a teaspoon of garlic and half a teaspoon of cayenne. I have a friend who puts onion powder, soy sauce, and ginger in his marinade.

When the meat is done soaking in the marinade remove and dry the strips of meat. Spread them in an electric dehydrator on the highest temperature setting, or in the oven at 140 degrees, and dry for approximately 8 hours. If the meat is raw and you're oven-drying, raise the temperature to 160 for about half an hour, then lower it to 140 for the remaining time.

Store in an air-tight container in a cool place. It doesn't have to be refrigerated, but try to use it within 3 months. Vacuum-sealing extends it's shelf life. You can cut the jerky pieces into chunks, reconstitute them in tepid water, and use them in casseroles, pot pies, and other meals.

Ground turkey is easy to dehydrate and is great to take along on camping and backpacking trips, or just to keep around the kitchen. I brown it in a pan, drain it and pat it dry, then spread it on racks and dehydrate it. As with jerky, vacuum-sealing will extend it's shelf life.

Freezing:

Turkey can be frozen either raw or cooked. Whole turkeys can be frozen in the plastic they're sold in, if you're freezing a store-bought turkey. If you are freezing turkeys you butchered yourself, be sure to wrap it well. Double-bag it, or use plastic wrap and freezer paper, or vacuum-seal it in freezer-safe bags. Cooked turkey can be removed from the bone and frozen in bags or containers, and the broth from cooking a turkey can be frozen in sealed bags or containers. Don't use glass because as the liquid broth freezes it expands, and the jar can break. Dry meat can be frozen in jars because expansion isn't an issue. Frozen turkey keeps well 6 months to a year, depending how well you wrapped it.

Salting/Brining:

Most salting and brining nowdays is used as a precursor to smoking the meat, but if you want to preserve a turkey for storage, you can use this method with caution. Whole turkeys are particularly troublesome because the salt/brine might not reach the deepest parts of the meat enough to draw out the moisture and keep nasty things like botulism from growing. If you're preserving a whole turkey it's safest to add a curing agent such as sodium nitrate (pink salt). It'll give the turkey a flavor reminiscent of ham, which is the curing agent used for ham and bacon. You can use these agents with pieces of meat too, for extra caution.

If your goal is preserving the meat and you don't care about keeping it on the carcass you can cut the meat into pieces and brine/salt it. Salting is a dry method of rubbing salt, either by itself of mixed with sugar and/or spices, into the meat. Brining is a wet method of soaking the meat in a very strong salt solution to which sugar and/or spices can be added. You can leave the meat in this solution for days, even weeks. If you're using raw meat it will still be raw meat and should be cooked before eating. Meat that was cooked before brining/salting is safe to eat right out of the solution. More information is in the section on salting and brining.

Smoking:

Smoked turkey is a classic favorite in the popular past-time of home-smoked meat. If you're hot-smoking the turkey it should be cooked first. For cold smoking you should brine the meat first, and if the meat is raw when you start, it still needs to be cooked before eating it. Brining and using curing agents, and then cold-smoking, will make the meat safe to store at room temperature for several weeks.

Pickling:

I have never pickled turkey, but supposedly anything that can be submerged in vinegar can be pickled. I'm not sure you'd want to pickle a whole turkey on the bone, so it might be best to debone it and then cover the meat with vinegar in a jar or crock.

Duck and Goose

Duck and goose kind of get a bad rap as domestic meat because waterfowl tends to be greasier than other poultry, and there isn't any true white meat. But there may be times when you need to preserve either wild or domestic water fowl.

Canning:

Duck and goose, like all meat, must be pressure canned. It is not safe to water-bath can duck or goose because the temperature doesn't get high enough to kill all the pathogens and bacteria. Please don't take a chance on sickening or killing anyone by water-bath canning duck or goose meat.

The meat of water-fowl is tastier if you add seasoning to it when you are canning it. You can soak the meat in a marinade, or simply add your seasonings to the jar when you put the meat in. I'm partial to putting teriyaki sauce in with goose. Some people use various meat marinade flavoring with water fowl. It's a matter of personal taste, but if your family thinks it doesn't like duck or goose, try spicing it up and see what they think.

Processing time and pressure for Duck and Goose:

Quarts:
70 minutes at 10 lbs pressure if you're less than 1,000' elevation
70 minutes at 15 lbs pressure if you're over 1,000' elevation.
Pints:
50 minutes at 10 lbs pressure if you're under 1,000' elevation
50 minutes at 15 lbs pressure if you're over 1,000' elevation

Dehydrating:

Duck and Goose meat can be dried, but it's not as lean as other poultry and the fats will make for a shorter shelf life. Cut the strips of cooked meat a little thinner than for leaner meats, cutting with the grain rather than against. This helps keep the meat from falling apart when you pick up the dried pieces.

Season or marinade the meat before drying. Make sure your drying temperature is around 140 degrees. It generally takes 8 to 10 hours to dry. Store in air-tight containers in a cool place, out of the light if your container is clear and allows light through it.

Freezing:

Duck and goose can be preserved by freezing, either raw or canned. Wrap well or place meat in air-tight freezer-safe container.

Salting/Brining:

Waterfowl can be preserved by salting and brining. It's usually combined with smoking but it is possible to preserve it for 2 or 3 weeks with a salt or brine cure.

Smoking:

Smoked duck is delicious. Start with a seasoned brine, then follow directions for smoking. If you plan to eat it within a few days, the hot-smoke method can be used, otherwise use the cold-smoke method to preserve it for a longer period of time.

Pickling:

It is possible, since nothing rules it out, but I've never known anyone who did it.

Oil:

There is an old-time method of preserving ducks and geese in their own fat or oil. The bird is cut up like you would a frying chicken, and the skin removed. Then it's salted or soaked in brine for a couple days, after which it's cooked at a low temperature, around 260 to 275, for several hours. The fat is rendered from the skin, and the cooked duck or goose is coated with it's own oil and stored in a crock in the coolest part of the house or in a basement or root cellar. It kept for months this way.

Fish

Canning:

Fish can be canned but more caution should be taken than with other meats. The processing time to kill the botulism-causing critters is longer. This can alter the color, flavor, and texture of the fish, but processing time should not be cut short. In my opinion the fish is still very tasty. If you want to pep up the flavor you can marinade your fish first, and even better, you can smoke the fish to add flavor, then can them.

Most fish should be fileted from the carcass before canning. The small bones can be left in, as you would for fresh cooking. Salmon is usually canned bones and all. In home-canning we cut the backbone away, but most commercial canned Salmon I've bought has had the backbone pieces in it. I sift through with my fingers and remove them, but leave the other bones. They soften and aren't even noticeable when you eat the Salmon, and they're a good source of calcium.

Do not cut the processing time short! Use pint jars if you don't want to process fish the longer length for quarts!

Processing time and pressure for fish:

Quarts:
160 minutes at 10 lbs pressure if you're less than 1,000' elevation
160 minutes at 15 lbs pressure if you're over 1,000' elevation.
(That's 2 hours and 40 minutes!)
Pints:
110 minutes at 10 lbs pressure if you're under 1,000' elevation

110 minutes at 15 lbs pressure if you're over 1,000' elevation

Dehydrating:

This is most successful with low-fat fish. High-fat fish, such as Salmon and catfish, can be dehydrated but you need to dry it longer and it's shelf life will be shorter. The finished product is pretty much Jerky, but can be a tasty treat. It's still possible to rehydrate and cook with it but it'll behave differently than fresh fish.

To dehydrate fish, cut the fish into thin strips, about 1/2" thick, keeping them as even as you can. Fish tend to taper off, so it's not always possible to have an even thickness the whole length. Soak the fish strips in salt water, about 1 cup salt to 2 cups water, for about half an hour. Remove fish, rinse, and pat dry. Next, put the fish in a bowl with salt and the seasonings of your choice, cover and gently shake to distribute the seasonings. Store in refrigerator or cold place over night. The next day, spread the fish out to dry. Use a hot temperature around 140 to 150 degrees. If you're drying fish near or over a fire try to keep the fire hot during the six to eight hours of drying time. Depending where your fish strips are hanging you may be smoking them at the same time, which is a common and ancient way of preserving fish.

When dry, store the fish in an airtight container in a cool, dark place. It should keep from a few months to several months, depending on the leanness of the fish. If you started with raw fish, remember that it is still raw. However, most fish will start cooking at a lower temperature than meat, so if your drying temperature was high enough, the fish is considered 'cooked' as well as dried.

Freezing:

Fish can be frozen the same as meat. Raw fish can change in texture when it has been frozen. The water content of fish is higher and as it freezes it can get large crystals of water in the meat, which can make the fish meat mushy and limp when thawed. Cooked fish won't have this problem, and commercially frozen fish is a faster process that avoids the water crystal problem.

Make sure fish is well-wrapped to prevent freezer burn. Double-bag it, or wrap it in plastic and then freezer paper, or vacuum-seal it in freezer-safe bags. If wrapped properly it will keep for months in a freezer. Thaw the fish for a day or two in the refrigerator before using. Remove the heads and any other parts you would normally remove before cooking, before you freeze the fish.

Salting& Brining

Salting and brining are mostly used in combination with drying and/or smoking fish. The fish is cut into strips or filets and layered with salt in a crock, barrel, or other container, or it's soaked in a strong brine solution. When an expedition was to go over sea or over land, the fish-layered-in-salt was a good way for them to transport it and have edible fish for several weeks. Brined fish still has to be dried or smoked, or both, to preserve it. If you leave it in the brine it will eventually ferment and you'll have pickled fish.

Lean fish absorbs the salt or brine faster and more thoroughly than fatty fish, and smaller pieces better than bigger pieces. Fish has a much higher percentage of water in it's flesh than other meats, and takes a stronger solution to remove the water.

Here is David's directions for salting fish, in combination with dehydrating: "*When I salt fish, I use fillets from lean, mild-flavored fish; no catfish, carp, or others that tend to have a strong, fishy smell or flavor. Just my preference. I chose not to work with 'bone-in' fish just because they are not as easy to work with and they will not fit into my dehydrator.*

The first step is to make the brine cure. I do this by dissolving enough water in a large basin to 'float and egg'. You should make enough of the liquid so that there will be enough salt dissolved to soak into all the fillets. Some sugar can be added to the brine for variety.

Then I make sure the fillets are completely clean, fully thawed, and have no ragged pieces attached to them. Small or ragged pieces will tend to fall off of the fillets and muck up the process.

Place the fillets into the brine, being careful that the container is not over-crowded and that it will hold enough brine to cover the fillets. I use a granite-ware baking dish that has a cover.

The fillets need to be soaked in the brine until they have 'firmed up'. They take on a firmness and texture that will hold it's shape and not bend like a limp noodle. This is referred to as being 'struck through' with the cure. For fillets about ¼-inch thick this should take about 24 hours.

The fish should now be placed in a strainer to drip dry. After they have dripped, towel-dry them by patting and place them onto your dehydrator trays. Dry them at a low heat, about 110 – 115 degrees until they are completely dry. Heats higher than 115 can cook the fillets while they are drying. Store in an airtight container.

Smoking:

Smoking fish goes hand-in-hand with salting and brining, with brining being the most common way to prepare fish for smoking. My son-in-law soaks the fish in a strong brine solution first, for about half an hour to an hour. Then he removes the fish from that solution and puts it in one with salt and seasonings, like a marinade, and lets it soak in the refrigerator over night. The next day he takes the fish strips out and places them in his smoker. At this point he hot-smokes them for a few hours and the heat also cooks them. They can be eaten right out of the smoker.

If you want to preserve them for a longer time it's best to use the cold-smoke method after brine-soaking. Keep the temperature under

80 degrees and smoke for 3 to 5 days.
You can use fattier fish with this process and the smoke will permeate the fat and give the fish a delicious flavor. However, although it will be moister and tastier than lean fish, it will not store as long. Store in a cool or cold place. Fish is one of the exceptions to air-tight. You can wrap it in paper or foil.

To make fish safer to store you can add sodium nitrite or other curing agents to the brine.

Pickling:

Soak the fish in a brine over-night, wash, pat dry. Mix white vinegar with salt, sugar, and your favorite fish spices and seaonings. Bring to a boil, then pour over fish. Cover and store in a cool place. Do not heat-process, such as in a canner, at this point because it will caramelize your pickles and give it a bitter flavor.

Oil:

Fish was sometimes preserved by covering it with oil in barrels or tightly-woven baskets before refrigeration was available.

Dairy

Milk

Some dairy products, such as butter, cheese, yogurt, and sour cream, are ways of preserving milk, and those foods can then be further preserved in other ways for longer shelf life. In this section I'm going to talk just about milk, and these processes apply to both store-bought and home-produced milk from any dairy animal.

Canning:

Milk can be poured into jars and canned, to be stored at room temperature until opened. It is low-acid and should be processed in a pressure canner. Some websites I looked at cautioned against canning milk because if it's not canned long enough and hot enough, it might not kill all of the botulism bacteria. I've done it for years and know several people who have. Does that make it safe enough for *you*? That's up to you. There are people and institutions that believe all home preserving of food is risky, yet few people are sickened each year by home-processed foods, by far, than by commercially processed foods. None of us wants to be the one who gets sick or sickens someone else.

The finished product will be a tannish color, like evaporated milk, and have a carmelized hint to the flavor, although not as strongly as evaporated milk. You can simmer the milk on the stove and evaporate water out of it, then can the milk as evaporated milk, but it's hard to know how thick the milk is and how much water would thin it back to it's original strength. It might not be important to have it exact; it just means the milk will be either weaker or stronger.

As far as I know and have personal experience with, it doesn't matter whether you use whole, 2%, 1%, or skim for your canned milk. The important thing is for the high temperatures produced during pressure canning to kill any pathogens in the milk. At first glance you would think that skim milk would do best, being thinner it would allow the heat to penetrate to the center of the jar. But the fat in whole milk could act as a transmitter of the heat to the center of the jar.

Store the cooled jars of milk in a dark place so the milk won't take on an 'off' flavor. If you plan to use the milk as a beverage be sure to chill it before opening. Room temperature milk is not as tasty as cold milk. I canned egg nog one year at Christmas time so we could have a treat the next summer. It worked fine, but I hadn't thought about chilling it and we opened it at July room temperature! After that we chilled the jars of egg nog before opening!

Milk, egg nog, or any dairy product with fat in it will separate during the canning process. A quick shake with the lid on tight will mix it back together.

Processing time and pressure for Milk (and egg nog):

Quarts:
25 minutes at 10 lbs pressure if you're less than 1,000' elevation
25 minutes at 15 lbs pressure if you're over 1,000' elevation.
Pints:
20 minutes at 10 lbs pressure if you're under 1,000' elevation
20 minutes at 15 lbs pressure if you're over 1,000' elevation

Dehydrating Milk:

This isn't something that is easily done at home. It takes too long to dry the liquid out of the milk particles. If you decide you really want to try it, I suggest simmering the milk first to reduce the liquid as far as you can. Use a dehydrator with stacking trays so you don't have to move them once you pour the milk onto it, and also a dehydrator with fruit leather trays that have a lip around the edge to hold in liquids. I have never tried this and I don't know if it would work, but if I were to experiment, this is what I would try first.

Freezing Milk:

Milk can be frozen, but when thawed it might be separated and grainy. You can shake it to mix the fat back with the water and that helps to some extent. It's drinkable as a beverage but if you don't like it that way after freezing, you can still use it for cooking and baking.

If you freeze it in a plastic jug set it upright and leave the lid most of the way unscrewed to allow air out of the jug, since the milk will expand as it freezes. Even then it's a good idea to set the jug of milk in a bowl or other container as it thaws in case the plastic of the jug has split somewhere and wasn't visible. Don't freeze milk or other liquids in glass jars.

A handy way to freeze milk is in ice cube trays. I measured mine once and each cube was ¼ cup. When the cubes of milk were frozen I dumped them out into a ziplock freezer bag. If I was baking or making gravy or anything that needed milk, I just took out however many cubes I needed to equal the amount of milk required.

Sugaring Milk:

David sent this delicious recipe for extending the shelf life of milk: "*This recipe is not intended to be a way to store milk long-term but it will increase the shelf life to days, and sometimes weeks, depending on the temperature. It was used South of the Border as a way to keep milk from spoiling in homes without refrigeration. In modern times it has become a dessert ingredient that can be swapped for Sweetened Condensed Milk.*

It can also be canned for long-term storage. I have never pressure canned it because it probably wouldn't survive the process. (It would probably turn into caramel sauce). *Water-bath is the only way I have canned it.*

Dolce de Leche

1 gallon milk
5 cups sugar
1 teaspoon baking soda (optional)

Mix the milk, sugar, and baking soda in a large pan and bring to a simmer on low enough heat that it does not scorch the milk. Stir occasionally.

The mixture will start to thicken and turn slightly brown after several hours. The browning will give it a slightly caramel flavor.

The baking soda raises the ph of the mixture slightly and will aid in the caramelizing of the milk.

When the mixture is at a desired thickness and taste, remove from heat and pour into jars and put lids on them.

You can reduce the measurements and make a half-batch or even a quarter-batch of this. It's so good that you'll wish you'd made a whole gallon though!

Salting, Brining, Smoking, and Pickling:

These are not used with milk as a method of preserving.

Butter

Canning:

Butter is easily canned, and can be processed in a water-bath canner or in a pressure canner. You can melt the butter in a pan and pour it into the jars, or you can cut the butter into pieces and fill the jars with them. With the second way, once the jars have some butter in them, set them in a pan and fill with hot water about halfway up the jars. Don't get water in the jars with the butter. You can set them on a stove burner on a very low heat setting and wait while the butter melts. As it does, add more butter to the jars until you have them filled, leaving at least half an inch of empty space at the top of the jar, to allow for expansion. This is called 'head space'.

One time I was in a hurry and just crammed butter into the jars and put them in the water bath kettle. I figured if I had enough butter in there it would still be pretty full when it was melted during canning. The butter came out okay but it took longer to bring the water to a boil in the canner kettle because it also had to do the job of heating and melting the butter. In the end I didn't save much time, and my jars were only about 2/3 full of butter. There was more air in there than I thought.

As the butter was melting you should have the canning lids simmering in a pan of water. This softens the rubber to help it make a good seal to the jar. When the butter is melted, or you have poured melted butter into the jars, wipe the rims with a clean, damp cloth, then fish a lid out of the hot water and place it on the jar. Screw a ring over it, then set the jar in the canner. Be sure everything is clean and sterile, especially with water-bath canning.

When all the jars are in the canner you're ready to start the processing. After processing and you have removed the jars from the canner, when it begins to cool shake the jars every five to ten minutes to mix it back up. Do this gently with a rocking motion so you don't make it frothy. Once it's cool it won't separate again.

Processing time for Water-bath canning butter:

Process pints and half-pints for 30 minutes and quarts for 45 minutes, timed from when the water starts boiling.

Processing time and pressure for pressure canning butter

Quarts:
10 minutes at 10 lbs pressure if you're less than 1,000' elevation
10 minutes at 15 lbs pressure if you're over 1,000' elevation.
Pints and half-pints:
5 minutes at 10 lbs pressure if you're under 1,000' elevation
5 minutes at 15 lbs pressure if you're over 1,000' elevation

Dehydrating Butter:

This is done commercially, mainly as freeze-dried butter. It can be gone at home but the finished product is more of a soft-spread than a hard butter. That's not necessarily a bad thing. I asked David if he had ever tried dehydrating butter... *"I have seen "Butter Powder" but have no idea how they make it. I have never put any in the dehydrator to see how it comes out but I'm sure there's more to it than just applying heat. Maybe mixing it with cornstarch and drying? I know what I'm going to be doing tonight – trying to dehydrate butter! Will get back to you tomorrow on what happened."*

"I was thinking about the butter powder and got to thinking that maybe powdered milk would work better than cornstarch. My line of thought was that cornstarch would tend to thicken anything that was cooked with the powder.

I mixed it all up and added just enough water to dissolve the milk, and it's in the dehydrator now. Because the water is bound in all that fat, it may take all night to dry. I don't know, but I will keep an eye on it.

It tasted just a little like powdered milk but I think the overall taste will be okay. If it doesn't work out the way I want it to, I'll try it with cornstarch tomorrow."

"I tried mixing some of the butter with only milk powder in it but it just clumped and wouldn't dissolve in the butter fat. It only blended in after I poured in a few cups of water. I melted 2 pounds of butter, mixed in 4 cups of milk powder, and 2 cups of water. It's starting to dry out now in the dehydrator and so far it tastes like it will have a decent flavor. If it has enough milk powder in it I think it will do okay."

(Next Day) *"I was pretty sure the butter would take a while because of the high fat content, but so far it looks like it just may turn out to be something workable. I'll know more after it finishes drying. I may have to redo the experiment with a little more milk powder. I think it may still be too oily to store. I'm thinking that to make a usable spread from it, we may be able to mix it with some olive or other good oil and use it that way. I'm sure it would be usable in cooking as it is right now, but I'll have to give it a try to find out for sure."*

(Later, same day) *"I took the butter out of the dehydrator a little while ago. It is still pretty oily and I don't know how it will store. I may have to do some more experimenting with it, "BUT!", I did try mixing some with oil and running it in the blender. The milk just clumped together like it did when I originally mixed it in to the butter. I turned the blender on and started dripping water in as it ran, and almost like an explosion, the whole batch of it turned white and thick like mayonnaise, instantly! It startled me!*

I tasted it and I do think it would make a good spread, but it is most definitely not butter or margarine. I tried it on a piece of fresh bread, on some boiled potatoes, and on some plain pasta – it wasn't bad. I would consider it a plus if I didn't already have fresh or canned butter available."

(Another 'later') *"I put the bowl in the fridge for a while and it set up just like a tub of soft-spread margarine. I tried a bit more of it on a piece of bread; now I know it's a winner! It melted in my mouth just like real butter, even though it's flavor wasn't a match. It would be especially good with chives or garlic mixed in, and used as a spread on fresh, hot bread or crackers."*

(Two days after that) *"I used some of the 'experimental' butter tonight. Made "Chicken n dumplins" out of the leftover cured chicken and put some on biscuits. It worked well on both, but on the biscuits it didn't melt. It stayed crunchy but the taste was good."*

(A few days later) *"I made a discovery tonight! I was going to make more of the 'powdered butter, and my mixing bowl was too small so I tried to use less water and the butter/powdered milk mixture just lumped up like a ball of bread dough when I mixed it with the beaters. It didn't feel overly oily and it didn't stick to my hands so I just pressed some of it onto the liners of the dehydrator trays and put them on to dehydrate.*

I had a crazy idea and mixed some of the remaining 'dough' up with water and ran the mixer in it until it was all dissolved and guess what? It was milk! Whole milk, no butter or oil anywhere, and it tasted better than the whole milk made with the Nido Whole Milk Powder.

That's not the only thing! I mixed a little less water with another lump and tried to whip it like whip cream and it's whipped. Not good and stiff like fresh cream but it was definitely whipped cream, no butter taste or butter fat floating anywhere.

<u>Freezing Butter:</u>

Butter can be frozen in the boxes it comes in from the store and keeps quite well for months. Leave the paper-wrapped sticks in the box. Alternatively, you can put the sticks in a different freezer container or vacuum-seal them.

Salting, Brining, Smoking, and Pickling

Not known to be used to preserve butter. If you must store butter at room temperature try to do it in an oxygen-free environment. There used to be butter keepers that were inverted in a matching bowl of water, which created a barrier between the butter and the outside air and it kept butter for weeks even in summer. Barring that, put the butter in an air-tight container and keep it in the coolest dark place you can find. If you already 'wax' cheese for storage, you might be able to 'wax' butter as well, but I've never heard of anyone trying it.

Cheese

There are several types of cheese but I'm going to break it down into 'hard' cheese and 'soft' cheese. This won't be a how-to on making cheese. It's about how to preserve the cheese so it'll 'keep' longer.

Canning:

Both hard cheeses and soft cheeses can be canned. You can use either a pressure canner or a water-bath canner but the finished product has a better taste, texture, and color if you use a water-bath canner. Make sure your jars and other supplies are clean, and for water-bath canning, that they are sterilized by boiling.

The nice thing about canned cheese is that it returns to it's consistency when it cools after canning. Cheddar cheese, for example, will be hard like fresh cheddar cheese and you can slice or shred it. When people first hear about canning cheese they often ask me if it will be like cheese dips, which have the consistency of thick pudding. No, a firm cheese will cool to once again be a firm cheese, and soft-ish cheeses like mozzarella will be firm with with a little bit of 'give'.

Every type of cheese I've canned comes out nicely. . When you freeze cheese it tends to crumble when you thaw and use it, but canned cheese is easy to slice or grate. I use jars with straight sides, such as wide-mouth pints, or half-pint jelly jars with straight sides. To remove the cheese simply hold it in hot water for a couple minutes, then use a knife between the cheese and jar to slide the cheese out. Slice or grate however much you need, then slide the cheese back into the jar, put the lid on it, and refrigerate.

Really-soft cheese like cream cheese won't just slide out of the jar.

However, it's one of the nicest cheeses after canning, and one of my favorites to can. You'll have to use a spoon or a knife to scoop out what you need.

To an cheese, cube the cheese and fill jars with the cubes. Set the jars in a pan and fill pan with hot water about halfway to a third of the way up the side of the jars. Don't get water in the jars with the cheese. If you accidentally do get some water in it, pick the jar up and carefully drain the water out. Then turn the burner on to a low heat and let the cheese melt. This takes a little longer than melting butter. Keep adding cubes of cheese as the cheese melts and settles. Leave about half an inch at the top of the jar for head space.

Meanwhile, make sure you have the jar lids simmering in a pan of water. When the cheese is melted and the jars are full, wipe the rims with a clean, damp cloth, take a lid from the simmering water and place it on the jar and screw a ring over it. Put the jar in the canner.

<u>Processing time for Water-bath canning cheese:</u>

Process pints and half-pints for 30 minutes and quarts for 45 minutes, timed from when the water starts boiling.

<u>Processing time and pressure for pressure canning cheese</u>

Quarts:
10 minutes at 10 lbs pressure if you're less than 1,000' elevation
10 minutes at 15 lbs pressure if you're over 1,000' elevation.
Pints and half-pints:
5 minutes at 10 lbs pressure if you're under 1,000' elevation
5 minutes at 15 lbs pressure if you're over 1,000' elevation

<u>Dehydrating Cheese:</u>

I have never dehydrated cheese other than cream cheese, although it's on my 'to do' list of things to try. David, however, has dehydrated several kinds of cheese and sent me a vacuum-sealed bag of dehydrated cheddar last summer to try. I emailed and asked him how he dried it.

"On the cheese, I did it two ways. The first was just to grate the cheddar and spread it on fruit leather trays and dry it over a low heat. As the fat seeps out you need to keep it blotted off. If your heat wasn't too high, the shreds will not be melted together. It needs to be spread on paper towels or other absorbent 'stuff" to soak off any remaining fat.

The second way was to use fat-free cheese. It really dehydrates easily and fast, and you don't have the 'fat' problem to deal with.

The cheese can be milled into a powder or run through a food processor/blender to make it easier to rehydrate, but it really isn't hard to cook with without grinding it. The full-fat cheese tastes better but the fat-free rehydrates a little better, so both ways are really pretty good."

Yesterday he had mozzarella cheese in the dehdrator and before bed time he emailed and said it came out good but that the low-fat would probably be less oily.

What about soft cheeses, like cream cheese, I asked. "*I don't have any fresh cream cheese in the house now, but I'll open a jar of home-canned and put it in the dehydrator. I think that the regular cream cheese will dry okay. We'll see".*

Next day: "*The cream cheese came out okay. I spread it on a fruit leather tray and dried it at about 125 – 130 degrees for about eight hours, and it came out crumbly and didn't have any extra fat or oil on it.*

The ½ pint jar of canned cream cheese I opened and used didn't dry into enough to do much with, but I took about half of it and poured equal parts of boiling water on it, mixed it, and let it sit for a while. It came out tasting pretty much like fresh. It was still a spread and wasn't as "stiff" as fresh.

With what was left, I vacuum-sealed it and it appeared to be okay. I don't think it will brick together to the point where it would be hard to rehydrate."

Well, I had a block of cream cheese on hand and I thought 'why should David be having all the fun?' I live off-grid and it's January, so we don't have enough daylight hours for the solar electricity to run my electric dehydrator this time of year. I do my winter dehydrating on shelves behind the woodstove. I put shelf brackets on the wall and I set the dehydrator trays right on the brackets. The air circulates and dries most foods in a short time but I hadn't tried anything like cheese there yet.

A couple days ago I set the block of cream cheese out on the porch in the 12-degree weather for about an hour. Then I sliced it thinly with my cheese slicer and carefully laid the cold pieces on the drying screens. The block made enough slices to fill one tray and half of another. I set them on the shelf brackets behind the woodstove, which in this cold weather is kept going pretty warm day and night, and by morning the pieces had dried hard enough I could pick them up by the end and hold them up like cards. They still seemed to have moisture in the centers, so I left them over the day.

The next morning the cream cheese was try. I could pick up the pieces by the edge and stand them upright, but if I was rough with them they crumbled into pieces. I got out the blender and put the cream cheese bits in and turned them into cream cheese powder. It smelled wonderful. I measured it and had ¾ cups of cream cheese powder, and then weighed it. The 8-oz block of cream cheese dehydrated down to 3 ounces of powder.

Today I stirred a tablespoon of the cream cheese powder with half a tablespoon of water. It was grainy at first and tasted sort of crunchy, which is the same experience David had. I set it near the woodstove and left it for about half an hour, then stirred it again. The particles had absorbed the water and I had a creamy mixture. I spread some on a biscuit leftover from breakfast and it was good. Oddly enough, there was a very faint taste reminiscent of the smell of scorched cardboard. Other than that it clearly tasted like cream cheese.

Freezing Cheese:

Cheese can be frozen but the thawed product is often crumbly and difficult to slice. It's great for cooking. Be sure to wrap it well. You can freeze it, unopened, in it's original wrapping, and if you're going to freeze it for the long-term then double-wrap it, or put freezer paper around it, or vacuum seal it in a freezer bag.

Salting & Brining Cheese

This is usually done before smoking or waxing cheese but it can be done just as a form of preservation. The brine mixture draws out moisture and changes the lactose to lactic acid. This slows down the growth of mold and bacteria, and also helps start the 'rind' to form on the surface of the cheese.

Mix up a strong brine mixture and add calcium to it. You can use whey, about a cup to a gallon of water. If you don't add calcium the brine will suck calcium from the cheese, which will eventually weaken the rind of your cheese. Keep the brine cool, but if you've just made cheese, put it in the brine while it's still 'warm' and it will absorb it better. The top surface of the cheese will float but you can't just weight it down like you do when brining meat. Sprinkle the top surface heavily with salt to dry out moisture and start forming the rind.

The length of time in the brine varies considerably, depending on the density of your cheese, the thickness of the pieces, the temperature of the cheese and of the brine. The general rule is 1 hour per pound for each inch of the thickness of the cheese. When you remove the cheese from the brine, gently pat it dry, then let it air-cure for a day or so, turning the pieces every so often. After that you can either wax it or let it air-dry further to create a good thick rind.

Waxing Cheese:

This information has been provided to me by my friend, J D Smith, who makes her own cheese and waxes it for storing, among the many other skills and talents she has.

"*Waxing cheese is not difficult, its as simple as melting and dipping or brushing it on to the cheese. Some dip, some brush and some do both. Brushing takes practice. Dipping is easy. If you are going to try to brush use a natural bristle brush. A synthetic brush will melt.*

Find an old pot because you will not be able to use it for anything else. Get a pot a little bigger so you can set the wax pot into it. You want to put water into the bigger pot and just simmer the water. put the small pot with the wax into the bigger one. Like a double boiler. Wax has a low flash point What that means is it can catch fire easily. Make sure you don't boil the water! You must watch the pot!

The cheese must be cold before you start to wax. Put it in the refrigerator. The wax sticks much better when cold. Make sure the cheese is dry before you start.

Once the wax has melted, dip the brush in the wax and start at the top. Brush a thin layer on and let it dry. Once dry Brush wax on the side and let it dry. Don't try to rush the drying. Once the side is dry do the bottom. If you are brushing you will need to put 4 or 5 layers on. Make sure the cheese is covered in the wax. If you leave even a small spot open unwanted bacteria will get in and spoil your cheese.

Dipping is easier and faster. Once the wax is melted dip the top of the cheese in the wax. Let it dry and do the same for the bottom as well as the sides. When doing the side roll it in the wax putting your fingers on the top and bottom so as to not burn your fingers or hand. Be careful the wax is very hot.

What wax to use

Cheese wax is the best. It comes in red, yellow, and black. You can find it in specialty shops or online. You can also use beeswax. Cheese wax and beeswax are very pliable which is what you want. It wont crack and let nasty bacteria in.

Please don't use candle wax not only is it not pliable it can crack and let unwanted bacteria in and spoil your cheese. Never use a hard wax, including paraffin."

Smoking Cheese:

This is best when done with cheeses that won't melt when a little heat is applied, such as hard cheese like cheddar, pepper jack, and swiss. You can smoke both store-bought or home-made cheese. Most modern cheese-smoking is done for taste and appearance, rather than for actual food preservation and storage. To smoke it for preservation purposes use the cold-smoking method and smoke it for several days. A minimum of five days is needed for the smoke to draw out moisture and seal the outside of the cheese so bacteria and mold won't grow, and you can smoke it for as long as a month is you like. Follow directions for brining in this chapter on cheese and also in the 'methods' section on smoking food. Store the smoked cheese in an airtight container or vacuum-seal it. Opinions vary on whether it needs to be refrigerated or stored in a cool, dark place.

"Aging" cheese is done at around 50 to 60 degrees, and is often done before smoking. Even commercial store-bought cheese can be aged and then brined and smoked. Some people won't smoke cheese that hasn't aged for at least 2 years. The advantage I can see, as a prepper, is that it's a great way to store cheese for that two years, assuming it wouldn't be eaten before then.

Pickled cheese:

This is considered a treat or a luxury in many parts of the world. The cheese is first brined, then put into a pickling solution along with spices and seasonings. My favorite recipe calls for cubing the cheese, soaking it in brine for half an hour, rinsing it, and layering it in a jar with thyme between the cubes. The vinegar is mixed with honey and heated, allowed to cool somewhat, and poured over the cheese. Provolone works well with this recipe. There are no exact measurements because I tend to cook by feel.

Simple cheese-making without rennet:

I know I said this book wasn't a 'how-to', but these simple cheeses can be considered a to be a way of preserving dairy products such as milk. They don't require rennet or fancy equipment or procedures, and anyone can do it. The following instructions were provided for this book by avid-cheese maker, J D Smith:

Soft cheese is easy to make. You will not need rennet to make these cheeses. All the cheeses must be put in a covered container in the refrigerator or some place cool. They will keep for 1 to 2 weeks. Once you have tasted these yummy cheeses they may not last the day.
With the exception of the Queso Blanco all are spreadable. The Queso Blanco is a solid cheese that does not melt. You can cut it up to put into soup or other dishes. Or you can roll the chunks in bread crumbs and fry them. (Susan's note: I'm going to try *this!* Yum! I love breaded cheese!)
You don't have to use cheese salt. You can use non-iodized table salt or no salt. Its up to you.

Soft cheese without rennet.:

Yogurt Cheese

1 qt yogurt
cheese salt

Get the yogurt to room temperature. Put the yogurt at room temperatur in a colander lined with butter muslin. Bring the corners up and tie it into a bag and hang to drain. Drain for 12 to 24 hrs to desired consistency. Remove from bag and add salt to taste.
You can add herbs if you like. Spread on anything that you like: bread, crackers, muffins.

Lemon cheese

1/2 Gallon whole milk
1/4 cup lemon juice

Heat the milk in a large pot to 190 degrees. Add the lemon juice and stir it well. Cover the pot and let it sit for 15 min. If it does not set add a little more lemon juice until it does.

Pour the curds in a colander lined with cheese cloth. Tie up and let it drain in the bag for a few hours. Put in salt to taste.

Queso Blanco

1 gallon whole milk
1/4 cup vinegar

Heat in a large pot 1 gallon milk to 190 degrees. Stir it or it will scorch. Add a little vinegar at a time. The curds will separate from the whey. Pour the curds in a colander lined with cheese cloth. Tie up and let drain 4 to 5 hours

Cottage Cheese

<u>Canning:</u>

I tried canning cottage cheese once, and so did David. We both had the same thing happen. The top third of the jar was a thick white mass and the rest of the jar was a clear liquid. It could be shaken and used in cooking for flavoring, but it didn't have much use otherwise. It's not the best way to preserve cottage cheese, but if you have no other way and really want a way to keep it 'edible' for longer storage, I'll give the times and pressure for it. It must be pressure canned and not water-bath canned because it's not acidic enough for water-bath canning. When I canned it I used pint jars and processed it for 60 minutes at 15 lbs pressure since my location is over 1,000' elevation. Below that elevation you can use 10 lbs pressure.

<u>Dehydrating Cottage Cheese:</u>

This works surprisingly well. It even reconstitutes to something close to fresh cottage cheese. I was going to give this a try but before we could get out to town my sidekick, David, went ahead and tried it with both regular and non-fat cottage cheese. He spread it on fruit leather trays and put it in his dehydrator. The next morning he wrote "*When I got up I checked the cottage cheese. The low-fat cottage cheese was done. The*
regular cottage cheese was crusted over and I had to turn it to finish it up."

Later he wrote: "*It looks like you came up with a winner! The cottage cheese dehydrated well and rehydrated okay. When rehydrated the curd was a bit firm. The longer it sits the softer is has gotten, but I don't think it will ever get as soft as fresh. The taste was comparable to fresh and it was definitely identifiable as cottage cheese.*

To rehdrate it I just poured about twice as much boiling water (by volume) to the dehydrated curd and let it sit. I stirred it every two or three minutes over 15 minutes while it cooled. I gave it a taste... not bad!

Even if you don't want to eat it with peaches it should still be good for cooking things like lasagne. I plant to try this and keep it on hand. David sent me a vacuum-sealed package of his dried cottage cheese and it looks pretty tasty. I can see myself storing this and other dehydrated cheeses in vacuum-sealed bags stacked in a sealed bucket in my root cellar. Our home is many miles from a store so it would be a real saver for us, but also useful if something interrupts the supply in the store, or a storm traps me or you or anyone else, at home.

Freezing cottage cheese:

Cottage cheese can be frozen, even in the container you purchase it in, but might be grainy when thawed. You can stir it and smooth it out some, and I would eat it myself, and have. It would work very well in cooking. If the cottage cheese is home-made, freese it in an airtight freezer container or vacuum-sealed bag.

Salting, Brining, Smoking, and Pickling: Not known to be used to preserve cottage cheese, though pickle relish or pickled fruits or vegetables can be stirred into cottage cheese for a tasty treat. Doing this does not preserve the cottage cheese though.

Yogurt, Cream, and Sour Cream

Canning:

To my knowledge, yogurt and sour cream cannot be canned. It isn't that they wouldn't be edible if you canned them, but they would not resemble the fresh product. The taste might be the same, and you could use it for cooking, so if you really want to store some and have no other way to preserve it, you could certainly do so. It would probably separate like cottage cheese does when canned, but you could shake it to mix it together again, at least to some extent.

I checked with David because you just never know what he has tried in that 'laboratory' kitchen of his: "*I have canned yogurt and sour cream. They don't really much resemble fresh but it can be used in cooking and tastes okay. Both separate into a lump of solid floating in when, but a vigorous shaking or mixing with a fork will mix it back up. I water-bathed it after finding that canning totally destroys it.*" Which brings another thought to mind. Canning would probably destroy the active cultures in yogurt. It would still be an edible product with calcium and protein and such, but the enzymes or probiotics would be dead.

There are small cans of commercially canned cream available for sale but I'm wasn't sure if home-canning would create a caramelized product similar to condensed milk. I couldn't turn anything up on an internet search other than being directed to the store-bought already-canned cream. Then I emailed David: "*Yes, I have canned cream. I water-bathed it and since it worked I never tried to pressure can it. I don't remember how long I boiled it for but my train of through would have been 30 to 45 minutes if the cream was room temperature when I filled the jars, and about 15 minutes longer if it was cold out of the fridge. I only canned it in half-pint jars.*

Dehydrating:

I bought a carton of sour cream and spread it on wax paper-lined dehydrator trays and set it on my drying shelves behind and above my woodstove. I set them to dry around 10:00 in the morning and by evening it was dry. I dumped it all into a cake pan, then into my blender and made it into a powder. The dehydrated sour cream is slightly oily and clumped a bit when I powdered it. A small bit stirred with water reconstituted to where if you didn't know it had been dehydrated you might not be able to tell. Because it is oily I would store it in an airtight container, preferably something impermeable like glass, and keep it in a cold, dark place and try to use it in within a few months.

Again I turned to David: "*I have also dehydrated yogurt. It worked but isn't my first choice of how to eat the stuff. It takes quite a while to soften up and loses a lot in the process. It can be used as a starter for new batches.*"

On that note, here is directions for one method of making yogurt, contributed by my friend, J D Smith. I like this one because as the yogurt cools the jars seal and you basically have canned yogurt that can be stored on a shelf:

"Yogurt is an easy thing to make. You don't need a 100-dollar yogurt maker to do it. Yogurt is good for you. Its easier to digest than milk, helps in the intestines and colon. Has protean and calcium. There are so many benefits I can't list them all!

What you will need"

1 gallon whole milk
1 cup cultured plain or vanilla yogurt

Two large pots
4 1 quart jars with lids
one cooler big enough to hold the 4 jars along with one gallon of water. You can use a Styrofoam or plastic cooler.
A kitchen thermometer.

First you will want to sterilize your jars. In a large pot put an inch or two of water in and then put in the jars, lids, and rings. Bring it to a boil and boil for 10 minutes with the lid on. Take the pot off the heat and leave the lid on until you're ready for the jars.

In the other big pot put in the gallon of milk and heat it to 190 degrees. Take it off the heat and let it cool to 120 degrees. You can put the pot in some cool water in the sink if you like. It helps cool it quicker.

Once its at 120 degrees take out a cup of heated milk put it into a 4 cup bowl and whisk in the cup cultured yogurt. Then put it all back into the pot and whisk it in very well. You will need to get the culture mixed throughout the milk.

Next you will want to get your jars, lids, and bands out. Careful, the jars are hot. Use a jar lifter or a pot holder. Put the jars on a towel so the jars don't crack or break because the counter is cool. Pour the mixture in the jars within an inch of the top. If you want you can spoon out the bubbles. Put the lids and bands on and set the jars into the cooler. Heat a gallon of water to 120 and pour into the cooler. Close the lid and put it into a draft-free place for 4 hours. Check your yogurt after the 4 hours. You should have thick yogurt. If you don't you can leave it in for up to 12 hours. Put it in the refrigerator to cool for 5 to 6 hours.

If you would like less yogurt half the recipe for 2 quarts. Half it again if you would like a quart."

Here's a simple way to make sour cream from yogurt, contributed by J D Smith:

You can use yogurt to make sour cream. You will need:

1 cup heavy cream or half and half or raw cream.
2 tablespoons yogurt
A container with a lid
A towel.

Mix the cream and yogurt in the container. Cover it with the clean towel. The reason you cover it with a towel is you want the gasses to escape. Set it in a warm place for 12 to 18 hours. You will know when its set when you tip the container and it pulls away from the side. Put it in the refrigerator for 6 hours. If it's thin put in a tablespoon of milk powder.

Eggs

Canning Eggs:

Believe it or not, eggs can be canned. When my husband was in the Marines they had canned scrambled eggs, but the only canned eggs I knew about was to boil and pickle them, then process them in a water-bath canner. But I didn't take into account for David and his experiments... "*Funny you should ask about canning eggs! I have canned them and they are, in my opinion, very good. You can also add different ingredients for what I call "Canned Omelets", but the ingredients should be ones that don't have a lot of moisture in them or it could make the eggs soggy.*

I just beat the raw eggs and fill the jars, no more than ½ bull because they really swell and they can boil out all over inside your canner. The last batch I did was pressure canned for about 40 minutes at 5 lbs. (Note from Susan: For those of us over 1,000' elevation we would use 10 lbs., for the same length of time). *When I first started canning them I water-bath canned them for 40 minutes, but got to thinking and thought I'd try pressure canning them to see how it came out.*

Both ways did well. The pressure canned jars tended to darken a bit and were kind of firm but tasted good. At one time I had jars done both ways on the shelf and some of the water-bathed jars turned a little green, but that is not unusual for eggs. It just means that some oxidation took place at some point in the process. When I was in the Army and we had chow in the field, the eggs were almost always some shade of green and they were still pretty good. (Green eggs and ham, anyone?)

To make the 'canned omelets' just put the ingredients in the bottom of the jars and pour the eggs in on top of them and can them. Some ingredients that worked well were:

Ham
Sausage
Cheese
Green Olives
Black Olives

Some that didn't work too well were peppers and onions. They have too much moisture in them."

Now that I know this I plan to give it a try. It's winter, though, and we're using dehydrated eggs right now. I'll probably wait until we have some fresh eggs, though I could rehydrate these and then can them... Nah!

To can pickled eggs, boil the eggs and remove the shells. Make a solution of vinegar and whatever seasonings or spices you want to put in with them (salt, peppers, garlic, cloves, etc.). Boil the vinegar solution, allow to cool slightly, then pour over eggs. This is the same way to make pickled eggs, only you then next process them in a canner. You can use a water-bath canner for this. Process them for 25 minutes after the water boils. Allow them to cool over night before checking to see if they sealed. Put any that didn't seal into the refrigerator.

Boiled eggs can be canned in a saltwater solution similar to brining. Pour the brine over the eggs and process for 25 minutes after boiling, in a water-bath canner. The eggs will turn a tan color but they'll still taste the same. Rinse in fresh water to remove some of the salt, but they will still be salty. They're good in egg salad, and anything else cooked eggs are added to. I've thought I would try them in stir-fry sometime.

Dehydrated Eggs:

This is something that both David and I have done. In fact, each of us was dehydrating eggs before we ever met. A few years ago I started dehydrating my extra eggs over the spring, summer, and fall. The main reason I did this was because from about November until March our chickens don't lay eggs up here in the cold north, with our short winter days. We didn't like having to eat store-bought eggs during the months our chickens weren't laying.

In the summer we gave eggs away to everyone we could push them off onto, and it seemed a shame to give away so many eggs, then have to buy them in the winter, as well as buying feed for the hens during those months too. We live off-grid with a solar electricity system, so putting lights in the chicken coop isn't an option. Winters are cloudy and the days are short, so we have to conserve electricity during those months.

Dehydrated eggs have the disadvantage that you have to use them as scrambled eggs. That means no fried eggs in the winter, but lots of really good and creative omelets. The dehydrated eggs can also be used in baking. I use one tablespoon whole dried egg to 1 tablespoon water to make one reconsitituted egg.

You can also separate the eggs and dry the whites and yolks separately. If you like to bake things that call for egg whites, like meringue, you can use the dried whites. The dried yolks can be reconstituted and cooked for eating, or used in baking.

My Nesco electric dehydrator came with one plastic liner for making fruit leather. I use it when I dehydrate eggs and I line the other trays with wax paper. I cut the hole out in the middle so it sits on the tray around the center opening, and I trimmed the edges leaving leaving extra paper so I could bend it up and form a lip around the edge so the egg wouldn't run off the trays. I'm careful with the wax paper and re-use it for several batches before having to cut fresh wax paper.

Each of these trays hold four eggs. If you have a different dehydrator you can experiment to see how many it holds. Break the eggs into a bowl and whisk them until the yolks and whites are evenly mixed, if you're dehydrating whole eggs. With the lined dehydrator tray sitting on the dehydrator, so you won't have to move it after filling the tray, carefully pour egg onto the tray. Move the bowl around the tray and pour until you have a good covering. You can use a spoon to further spread it.

You don't want it to be too thick or it'll take a long time to try. I pour mine about the thickness of a plain chocolate candy bar. Try to spread it evenly so that you don't have part of the tray finished before the thicker parts are done. If your dehydrator has a temperature control turn it up to 135 degrees or close to that. You can dry eggs in the oven on a low temperature setting, but use the lowest setting your oven has. You don't want to cook the eggs, you just want to dry them. If you live in a dry climate you can air-dry the eggs. Watch them closely and pour them thinly on the trays. I tried flipping mine partway through to dry them faster and it was a messy disaster.

About an hour into the drying process you'll see a skin starting to form on the eggs. It takes my dehydrator about eight hours to dry four trays of eggs. When they're done I lift the wax paper off the dehydrator tray and turn it upside-down over a cake pan. The dried eggs should peel off without leaving a mess on the wax paper other than an oily residue and a few crumbs. You can lift an edge of the dehydrated eggs and check before dumping it in the pan. If it's still wet and slimy put it back on the dehydrator tray and dry it longer.

The dehydrated egg pieces will look like peanut brittle without the peanuts. As you crumble them up they resemble cornflakes. You can put them in the blender now and make egg powder, or pack them into a jar as crumbles and pack them down with a spoon as you fill the jar. I can fit four dozen dehydrated eggs into a quart jar. Imagine that... 48 eggs reducing to fit into a quart-sized jar!

If you have trouble re-hydrating the dried eggs try using different temperatures of water. I've found it doesn't behave the same each time I use it. It might look grainy when it's reconstituted but when you cook it as either scrambled eggs or omelets, it comes out with an even texture and a big spongy rather than fluffy. The taste is the same as fresh eggs. In baking I add the dehydrated eggs to the dry ingredients, then add an equal amount of water to the wet ingredients, rather than soaking it separately.

David dehydrates eggs pretty similarly but he does have a few differences: *"When I dehydrate them I do stir the eggs (sometimes, not always) about once every couple hours. I make sure that I don't try it until there is a good thick crust on the mixture so there will be less of a chance of spilling any of the liquid. It doesn't seem to do any good or harm, I just tend to be impatient and sometimes have a problem keeping myself out of things that should be left alone!*

I do dehydrate some whites and yolks separately and have made meringue from the whites, and mayonnaise from the yolks. We like Mayo and that's why I first started drying them separately. Then I discovered that the whites made good meringue, so I made sure I had a quantity of both packed away.

I went one step further with the powdering. I ran the crumbles through the grain mill and ground them to an extremely fine powder. When they are done this way the powder is fairly dry and not oily, but it's a pain to do. They always clog the grinder and you have to keep digging and poking to keep them feeding freely to the auger."

Freezing Eggs:

Eggs freeze nicely. Remove them from the shells first. I've seen directions that say you should separate the yolks from the whites, or stir them and then freeze them. But I've frozen them in custard cups straight out of the shells, and when they thaw they act like fresh eggs, yolks intact. Once they're frozen I dump them out of the plastic custard cups and put them in a big ziplock freezer egg. Another way to do this is to use ice cube trays, and either leave the eggs in them or dump them into a bag or other freezer container once they're frozen.

Salting & Brining:

With this method the eggs are placed in a jar, uncooked, and covered with a brine. You have to make sure there aren't any cracks in the shells. Mix a solution of 4 cups water and 1 cup salt and heat slowly until all of the salt dissolved. Cool slightly, then pour over eggs. Screw lid on and set in a cool place for a week to three weeks. The longer the eggs sit in the brine the saltier they'll be.

Leave the eggs uncooked until you're ready to eat them. Then boil and peel. They will be *very* salty. Some people prefer to use them in soups and casseroles, and not add other salt to the dish. Duck eggs and other eggs can be used besides chicken eggs.

This doesn't really get you more shelf-life for your food storage than simply keeping the fresh eggs in a cool, dry place. We've kept eggs in our root cellar for 3 months without spoilage. The times I found while searching the internet ranged from 10 weeks to three and a half months for eggs kept between 30 to 40 degrees. Our root cellar stays between 40 and 50 for most of the year, and we were able to keep eggs for 3 months.

When breaking open an egg that has been stored, break it into a separate bowl. That way if it's bad you don't lose the whole dish or pan of whatever you're cooking. You just have one egg to throw out and one bowl to wash.

Smoking:

I found a website where a man said he had coated some eggs with liquid smoke to see if it would preserve them. It broke down the calcium in the shells and he was left with eggs that had only the soft inner shell and they were very fragile.

Eggs can be smoked with the cold-smoke method but it is only a flavor-enhancer and not a means of preserving or extending their storage or shelf life. Use unpeeled soft-boiled eggs and leave them in the smoker for half an hour to an hour an a half, depending how much smoke flavor you want in the eggs. They make great potato salad and deviled eggs.

Pickled Eggs:

Pickled eggs are standard fare in a lot of parts of the country, and I'm sure there are local variations and lots of recipes for them. Some people put the spices and vegetables in the jar with the eggs, then boil the vinegar and pour it the contents of the jar, and other people put the spices and vegetables in the vinegar and bring it to a boil, then pour the whole mess over the eggs in the jars. Either way, screw the lids on and set aside for a minimum of a week. If you plan to keep them unrefrigerated for longer than a week, you might want to process them in a water-bath canner for 25 minutes.

Here's a recipe for Pam's Pickled Eggs. She says she likes to use Banty eggs because they're the right size to just pop a whole egg in your mouth. And this is sure a mouth-watering recipe!

Mustard Pickled Eggs:
12 or more bantam hard-cooked eggs, peeled (enough to fill jar)
1/2 teaspoon mustard powder
1/4 teaspoon mustard seeds
1 1/2 teaspoons cornstarch
1 teaspoon white sugar
1/2 teaspoon ground turmeric

1 teaspoon salt
2 cups apple cider vinegar

Place the hard-cooked eggs into a 1 quart jar. In a saucepan, stir together the mustard, cornstarch, sugar, turmeric, and salt. Pour in just enough of the cider vinegar to make a paste, then gradually stir in the rest. Bring the mixture to a boil, stirring frequently. Pour into the jars with the eggs and mustard seeds. Put the lid on the jar, and refrigerate for a few days before eating for best flavor.

Other ways to preserve eggs:

There are old descriptions of egg preservation that call for dipping the eggs in wax, rubbing them with butter, storing them in a gel-like substance, packing them in sawdust, and anything that would create a barrier to keep bacteria from permeating the egg shell. A caution I would offer if you are going to try any of those methods is to remember that the egg shell is porous and anything you put on the outside is going to work it's way inside the egg shell. If you use something like vaseline to coat the outside, remember that washing it off won't remove it entirely. When you eat the egg you will be ingesting small amounts of whatever you exposed the shell to.

Conclusion

I hope you've found this book interesting and have learned one or two things along the way. If you have comments or suggestions, or want to read more food storage or preparedness related information, please visit our blog at:

http://www.povertyprepping.blogspot.com

The blog was created as an addition to my other book, "Poverty Prepping: How To Stock Up For Tomorrow When You Can't Afford To Eat Today". I answer reader questions and post suggestions, and there are a few regular guest columnists that post preparedness, homesteading, gardening, or food processing information, along with the information I post.

It's not a commercial site and it's free for you to visit as often as you like. Other than having links in the side bar to Amazon and to my other books, there is no advertising. The information is on the blog for everyone to learn from, and it keeps growing as we add more.

You can also email us at: povertyprepping@yahoo.com

Thank you!

Other books by Susan Gregersen

Non-fiction:

Food Storage: Preserving Fruit, Nuts, and Seeds
(With David Armstrong)

Poverty Prepping: How To Stock Up For Tomorrow
When You Can't Afford To Eat Today

Life Without Refrigeration

Food Self-Sufficiency: Reality Check

Food Storage: Bug-out Buckets, Specialty Buckets, and Transition
Buckets, for Preppers

Fiction

A Tale of Two Preppers
The Long Ride Home-canned
They Rally Point
A Funny Thing Happened When We Took Back America
Over the River and Through the Woods
Back Across the Pond
The Double

36821800R00070

Made in the USA
Middletown, DE
12 November 2016